Breakout:

A Search For Being

Breakout:

A Search For Being

L. R. Wright

Fine Tooth Press

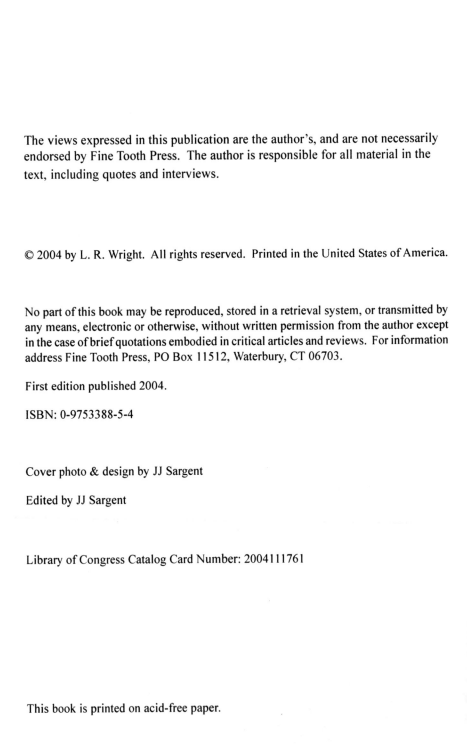

The views expressed in this publication are the author's, and are not necessarily endorsed by Fine Tooth Press. The author is responsible for all material in the text, including quotes and interviews.

First edition published 2004.

ISBN: 0-9753388-5-4

Cover photo & design by JJ Sargent

Edited by JJ Sargent

Library of Congress Catalog Card Number: 2004111761

This book is printed on acid-free paper.

In memory of the late Richard Lewis Wright

FOREWORD by Yvon Cormier, July 2004

Breakout (Breakout: A Search for Being) will come to be known as a seminal work in African-American literature as it further exposes the imposed separation between black and white cultures. At the same time, it deals with the social side effects of the slave era on black Americans in current times. This work revisits the unaddressed psychological scarring which has to date imbued black Americans, as individuals and as a community, with a blurred sense of identity. L. R. Wright and his companion's unique position of scaling both white and black worlds offers insight into clearing this clouded perception.

Wright introduces a variation on W.E.B. Dubois' "Double Consciousness," revealing meta-levels of separation, not just from white people but also among black peers. This even extends to mental division, where one's mind is divided against itself. This intimate recounting invites readers of all backgrounds to a view of reality divided between America's cultural pathology of racism, materialism, and a black man's striving to address his own and other people's humanity.

It is an autobiographical novel, revolutionary in concept, and without affectation. Wright's quest for meaning and identity gains formation by way of shared experiences with a voice of confirmation, his friend "Alan" (the real name has been changed for the purpose of providing anonymity). The basic root of understanding one's experiences is through a question and answer exchange of ideas. Historically referred to as "call and response," this motif is tied in with the traditions of the blues and the black American church. Leaving categories behind, Wright and Alan are having a personal conversation touching upon the universal aspects of a malformed culture, a conversation that queries a new approach in hopes that the American experiment will not fail due to its hidden iniquities.

Questions of what the "American Dream" really is, whether it includes materialism, racism or a social contract which only applies to white people or consumers, are in play. One of Wright's authorial antecedents is James Weldon Johnson's *Autobiography of an Ex-Colored Man*. Wright, like Johnson, exposes the contradictions inherent to Democracy which black Americans face – yet a century later. His other antecedent is Ralph Ellison's *Invisible Man*. As with Ellison, Wright expresses the full complexity of black life in all its facets relating to educational opportunity, taboos, questions of selling out, and what success is – without it either being written to a white or black audience.

Wright's work will shake people from the mental slumber of the American nightmare – a nightmare where "separate but equal" really means segregated and unequal. He discusses the possibilities of being a whole human being, negotiating one's existence, and holding America to its promise of equality beyond the given mixed blessings thus far. He chooses to shed his invisibility by addressing what gave it life.

An everyman's novel with a twist, *Breakout* leaves the reader knowing that asking the avoided questions and being true to one's self is a constant, even if there are no final answers. Rather than archetypes and moral constructs, *Breakout* breaks through barriers and adversity by providing the axis of fearless communication – though ephemeral today, this candor is needed in 21st Century literature. *Breakout* is the exchange between two individuals who seek to open their dialogue to everyone – reaching beyond misperceptions toward humanity.

Breakout:

A Search For Being

What's the Question?

On Tuesday, December 2, 1997, I broke the fuck out of New York, again; the start of yet another journey. For the previous 11 years, I had always been on the move, and then would settle down; just get the hang on things where ever I happened to be at the time, only to uproot again. This last upheaval was different, though. It was more intentional, more deliberate. This time around, I had a real sense of purpose. I was lookin' for something, but I didn't know exactly what I was lookin' for.

At the very least, I knew I was lookin' for some form of permanence in this last exit. I think Moms realized this as she dropped me off at the Port Authority Bus Terminal on 42nd Street and Eighth Avenue. I was ecstatic, anticipating a freedom I hadn't felt in 26 years of life. She had a look of worry and sadness drawn on her prettier than average, 52 year old face. I assured her there was nothin' to worry about. I was fine, or rather; I'd *be* fine, even though nothing was planned. I had no job lined up, no idea what I would do. All I knew was that I had a friend in Chicago I could stay with for a while. And I knew I had to go.

The surface reasons for leaving home were fairly obvious. I was tired of still livin' in Moms' one bedroom apartment in the Bronx. I was tired of sleepin' on the couch. I was tired of wondering if there was more to life than the usual routines of the consumer culture we now take for granted. I was tired of temping for far less than what you'd think a master's degree holder should earn. I was tired of mere simplistic survival in one of the fiercest cities in the world, always longing for something more and feeling weird that not very many people I knew felt that same urge to break out. I was tired of bein' tired.

But there was a lot more goin' on than just the typical frustrations of an unemployed, still- living-at-home idealist who had no idea what he wanted to do with his life. A question mark had built itself inside my head, even though I couldn't find the words to actually formulate the question. The build-up became unbearable after I attended a reunion of my high school's participation in an educational program called ABC: A Better Chance. ABC provided me with an opportunity to get out of the Bronx, attend high school in the affluent suburbs of Philadelphia, and step through doors which afforded me opportunities for further education, and, presumably, financial and social elevation.

At the reunion, the question mark that buried itself inside my head exploded into anger and resentment. Why, after having graduated from Georgetown University and receiving a graduate degree from Fairfield University, did I feel like I wasted my time and energy? Why didn't I feel as successful as I was supposed to feel with degrees from prestigious schools? Why didn't I have a "good" job like the other alumni at the reunion? Why wasn't I commanding a decent salary in any field or career? Why didn't I even want a fucking career?

I felt like I had been an experiment in the lab of Social Engineering 101. I resented the idea that I was supposed to be this "smart," black student who had the privilege of going to predominantly white, affluent schools, chasing the American Dream with more of an advantage than other black people, and that I was supposed to be grateful for this. Part of me wanted to consider myself privileged for having gotten those opportunities, but there was something else stirring inside full of bitterness. I felt like shitting those experiences out; one of those shits that takes up a whole roll.

Walking through the door that the ABC program opened for me, I set me off on a search for the ideals of success and achievement, goals that I had been taught were difficult for a minority like me in America to achieve. It seemed like the ultimate stroke of good fortune that a young black adolescent from the Bronx would have an easier go at "making something of himself." But as I looked around myself at the reunion, I didn't like what I was supposed to be making myself into: the middle-class black man, the carbon copy of well-to-do whites without the privilege of true equality because the race game is still in play, a game of hide and seek where everyone seemed blind, or even worse, acquiesced to the implicit program that codes certain ways to think and live, and all we can do is adjust accordingly like good pod boys and pod girls. It all seemed like an illusion.

After the reunion, I felt like I had just come down from a bad acid trip, a mickey slipped into my Kool Aid ten years earlier. I felt like my being and sense of purpose had been tricked by the trappings of what it means to be a "promising, black student" in America, of what it means to be black in America, of what it means to be an American, and what it means to just simply be. I needed to break out.

Seven months later, with this existential crisis in mind, I said goodbye to everybody in New York and hopped a Greyhound to Chicago with seven Benjamins in my pocket and a lot of shit on my mind. I didn't choose Chi-town 'cuz I enjoy freezing my ass off but because I had a good friend there who I met at Georgetown. Alan and I had a tight bond, one where we wouldn't speak to each other for a year or so, yet when the phone rang, we picked up right where we left off. We've had similar experiences and share a similar thought process. We're both African-American men who went to predominantly white schools. We both negotiated the complex, precarious racial line that separates the college social scene and America itself. We were both huge fans of the artist I'll forever refer to as Prince. When we were back in school, we didn't talk much about the things that drew us together. We didn't need to. We partied together, lived together, took classes together, and shared the usual glories and pitfalls of college life.

I knew I could trust him in light of the shit that was goin' on in my head. I knew he'd at least be sympathetic. But I also had a strong suspicion that our lives were fairly parallel at that point. I got this feeling when I called him from New York and asked if I could stay with him for a while. I was worried that staying with him for an indefinite period of time would cramp his style, but he said that he'd actually be grateful for the company. That's when I knew he had some shit on his mind, too. Cyclical periods of loneliness are inherent in the lives of seekers, and even though I really didn't know it at the time, Alan is definitely a seeker like me.

It had been three and a half years since I last saw him, but when I got off that bus, it felt like it was just yesterday I had last heard that unique, hearty, high-pitched, good-time laugh of his. I immediately felt like I was at home with him. It was good to know that we'd have time and space to catch up on the last three and a half years. It was good to know that he'd introduce me to his city, the place he loved so much but which I could only grudgingly appreciate with a New York state of mind. It was good to know he'd be proud to take me around his stomping ground. It was good to know he wouldn't charge me for rent.

It was an ideal situation for me to sort things out for myself. We were close friends separated only by distance. I felt less self-conscious of my thoughts and myself when I was around him. He knew all too well the things people like us went through in school, in work, in love, in life. It was the opportunity I was looking for to come to some kind of understanding of this thing I was lookin' for. I knew he'd be supportive.

Up until then, the only way I could try to deal with my thoughts about my experiences was to write. I wrote short stories in dribs and drabs, spurts of emotionally packed hyper-drama, hiccups of safe fiction, safe in the knowledge that I could express myself under the guise that 'This isn't really me.' I told Alan that I had wanted to write a book about my experiences. He thought the idea was great, but I wasn't convinced that it'd be worth anything to anyone. Why should anybody empathize with this schmuck who's pissed off about opportunities lots of folks don't have? Why should anybody care? What would I say that hasn't been said before?

The questions in my mind became obstacles as much as they were motivators, but with Alan's encouragement, I was able to start taking the task seriously. We felt like we hadn't heard enough voices from guys like us, African-Americans who were looking for new possibilities of shaping our identities beyond the usual race/ class categories forced on us by a this or that culture. Our experiences have lent us the ability to look at the world from both "black" and "white" perspectives. Our way of looking at the world, as so-called minorities, is a sort of double minority point of view; part of, but separated from, many of our black peers, and not just strictly concerning race issues. It was more about life issues: how we define ourselves and our purpose in this life, not just as black men, but as whole human beings.

In the days following my arrival in Chicago, Alan and I vibed on these issues of identity and purpose. In one of those rare moments of awareness, an idea slammed me. Alan is one of the most insightful, articulate, expressive people I've ever known. I wanted to include him. And the truth was that I needed pages. I needed ideas. I needed someone else to say what I was too blocked to say.

I asked him if he would let me invade his mind and claw at personal things, things he would not have talked about with anyone else, and put to word his harbored thoughts and feelings. I asked him if he would let me complement my story with his own. At this point, I thought my idea was too good not to do. Thankfully, he agreed without the slightest bit of hesitation. He saw it as a cathartic opportunity. He was just as excited as I was.

I spent the next 3 months interviewing Alan, recording our conversations with a hand-held tape recorder I bought just before I left New York. I asked as many questions as would come to mind about his life, his feelings, and his opinions on the issues that plagued me, questions concerning self-identity and self-purpose; how people like us related to others, and to ourselves, given our experiences as black men coming of age in predominantly white environments. I needed to formulate words that would fill in the blanks left by the question mark that built itself into my mind.

As I dug away at Alan through several hours of taped conversation, I dug deeper into myself, pulling out the weeds that irritated my being. I was diggin' away to get to that thing I was lookin' for but couldn't identify.

I condensed our conversations into a narrative form, leap-frogging his story with my own. There were lots of things I didn't know about Alan, things that, in our school days, I didn't need nor have the consciousness to ask about. But hearing his story helped me unlock doors within myself, doors I had either barricaded or had long forgotten about.

I'm eternally grateful for his courage. It was through his self-examination that I came to an understanding of my own. That thing I was looking for was inside of me, buried underneath my own story, unattended thoughts I hadn't yet processed. I began to peel away at myself, examining the creepy crawlies lurking inside, the things that made me cranky and unhappy, feelin' like I was somehow outside the norm, a black man who just didn't see things the way he had been taught to see them, a human being struggling to find his path amid the din of race and class confusion that keeps us separated from each other, and from ourselves.

This isn't meant to be a social dissertation on issues of race, class, history, education, or the mixed blessings of affirmative action. This isn't meant to be an indulgent autobiography, either. It's all of that, but something more. This is pointing to that thing I was lookin' for, the same thing I think we're all looking for at some point in our lives, the thing that might just point us in the direction of a hopeful future as individuals, as a nation, and as a community of nations. Answers are usually hard to come by, but it's the question that really burns. It was the question that pushed me forward all along. It started in the Bronx.

Lee's Are Played Out

I'd love to be able to tell you that I'm from mean streets, poor and needy, to feed the Horatio Alger in you and me, the po' boy making it good story that everybody loves to hear; the kind that soothes a guilty, liberal conscious like Vicks on a sore throat. But I don't come from rough streets. I'm not a street kid.

I love the Bronx. There's nothing bad I'd say about it to make it seem like I come from struggle and strife. A lot of "inner-city" folks like to wear their street ness like a badge of honor, to prove how tough they are, looking for their little doggy biscuit of respect. I'm not a hard-luck case. I was never hungry. My folks worked hard, no doubt, but they didn't have to sharecrop to fulfill my wants and needs. I went to private school first through fifth grade. I had enough money to buy Garbage Pail Kids cards, Bazooka Joe, and X-Men comic books. I was usually decently dressed, except for this one Easter Pops made me wear this ridiculous, green-as-grass, ugly ass Sixty's polyester suit to church. Besides that, I was spoiled silly.

Every Christmas was like heaven. Me and Lydell, my brother who's six and half years older than me, got everything we wanted and more: every Stars Wars action figure, two if they were soldiers, guards, or Stormtroopers, and almost every vehicle and playset. We got three-foot tall, giant Shogun warriors with wheels on their feet and plastic rocket launchers that could shoot you blind. Real fuckin' toys. Mickey Mouse weeble-wooble playsets. Electric Hess trucks. Marvel and D.C. comic book superhero and villain dolls with the nylon costumes that ripped too easily. Giant Godzilla with the shooting hand (Finally, something that could fight the Shoguns). The least disappointing Christmas was the one after the folks separated and bro left the house, when I had to accept a lone Atari 2600 system, a year after it had already been out, with PacMan and Donkey Kong.

But all in all, I was lucky. First of all, having been born to Richard and Timmie Lou Wright was luck. I never thought about the fact that they had to work to put me in private school and to inspire my imagination with all the toys I could cram into a rickety, wooden toy box. I was lucky to move out from the Mitchell Projects in the South Bronx to the Soundview section. I was lucky to have a variety of friends, all ethnicities, and even a gay dude, I think. I'm sure his sweet ass came out by now.

We dug Matchbox-car cities in the dirt when no one had a playset. We played "Off-the-Barrel," kinda like baseball, hitting the ball off of a big cement barrel instead of using bats. We played in the little park next to our apartment building because our folks wouldn't let us go across the street to the big park. We had our own Star Wars adventures. Marco, the blond kid next door, was always Luke. I was always Han Solo, before I was politically savvy enough to entertain the idea of being Lando Calrissian.

As far as I was concerned, my family lived large, working class with middle class ambitions. Pops had a high school diploma and worked at the Krasdale food plant in Hunts Point, when a man could still earn a decent living as a blue- collar worker. Moms started college but left, after becoming pregnant with Lydell, and worked downtown in banking. My folks had every intention on grooming me Lydell and me to be more than blue-collar workers. Education was their number one priority for us. For some reason, bro didn't go along with the program and chose a different path, becoming yet another statistic in the system. In a way, I hardly knew him. I didn't think too much about his destiny after he broke out, this coming on the heels of a visit by cops who were looking for him as a suspect in the burglary of our next door neighbor.

This happened shortly after the folks separated, so really, I was an only child from age 10 or 11 on. As my family fell apart, I didn't let it bother me too much. I suppose it's because my folks always played active roles in my life, regardless of which one I lived with. A therapist might say I fought my mental battles with my toys. I lived with Pops for about a year and a half after the separation and then moved in with Moms to the northwest Kingsbridge section of the Bronx. Pops moved downtown to 140th Street between Seventh and Lennox, the heart of Harlem. Most Fridays, when I was living with Moms, I'd spend the night out with Pops, either at City Island in the Bronx for shrimp and scallops, or he'd buy fresh shrimp from the market and cook'em at his apartment while I peeled and cut the potatoes for home fries. Then, off to the last show at Whitestone Cinemas, whatever movie I wanted to see. I always worried that we wouldn't get there in time for previews. He always got us there just in time.

He was a bad motherfucker before I ever heard of Shaft or George Thoroughgood. Nobody had shit on his straight-backed, proud gait; afro cropped short on the sides and puffy on top. His green and black dashiki hung loosely over his barreled torso. His mirrored shades cloaked the intention in his eyes. His expensive leather shoes clacked loudly on the sidewalk, forewarning his arrival on the scene.

I was a kid. It was all very dramatic to me.

From my scrawny point of view, he was intimidating, the classic, biblical, "fear thy father" thing made into reality. I understand now that he had other sides to what I assumed to be the stern, take-not-shit authority figure. He was laid back, passive-aggressive, and affectionate, traits that remind me of myself. He had no problem with hugs and kisses on the cheek, the scruff of his beard punctuating my annoyance. He wasn't afraid to say, "I love you." I was compelled to return the affection half-heartedly, as best as a kid could, a kid who really didn't understand what father-son love meant. It's not that I didn't love him; it's just that I didn't think that's how boys were supposed to talk to each other.

We had many a discussion on the finer points of life, most of which I can't remember, to my own disadvantage. I only remember him once referring to a Prince song on the radio.

"See son? He's tellin' her to act your AGE, not your shoe size. And you know women's shoe sizes don't go past nine!"

I've seen him run the gamut of emotions, from the belt-wielding madman who administered his sentence the two times he actually *caught* me fuckin' up, to the times when he just stared off into space in sad contemplation, looking for the next words to give me as Mr.Dear Abby.

"Son, I might not be able to leave you with much, but I can tell you..."

I can remember seein' him cry only once, at great-grandma Nana's funeral. It was one of the many down-south drives to St. Augustine, Florida, my folks' hometown. I didn't have access to the sadness of the occasion, being only eight or nine years old. I just knew that I was gettin' outta school a week before Christmas vacation to see aunts, uncles, cousins, and Grandpa Poppa Stoppa. I remember liking Nana, and I knew that I wouldn't see her again.

There must've been a bit of confusion on my face, not because she was gone, but because I had never seen my father cry before. I only looked him in the eyes once during the funeral, embarrassed to see him cry. It was one of those glances you sneak, like when you're compelled to catch a look at somethin' you're no supposed to look at. It wasn't sneaky enough because he was looking at me the whole time. When our eyes met, he smiled.

I hated seein' him cry. I hated that I wanted to cry because he was cryin', but I didn't. I didn't want him to ever see me cry, except for when he skinned my ass. Ass-whuppins' don't hurt as much as the fact that your ass is gettin' whupped. I cried more because of that.

I hate for anybody to see me cry.

I didn't cry the first time I heard my folks arguing. I didn't cry the first time Pops didn't come home for Christmas. I didn't cry at Moms' sadness of the whole thing. I didn't cry when Moms moved out.

I didn't cry as my family disintegrated. I pretty much tuned it all out and sunk into Star Wars action figure battle therapy.

Life became a bit more stressful after the separation. They both had to fend for themselves, so private school was out of the question. Sixth grade at I.S. 47 near Parkchester, in the Bronx, was my rude introduction to the New York City public school system. Most of the kids had gone to school with each other for most of their lives. I was the new, ex-private school brat, a prime target for merciless pre-teen teasing, and a fresh, juicy target for kids who were left back, two, three times. I never got beat up, but you know how fucked up kids can be. I think I would've rather gotten beat up than to be made to feel like an outcasted freak.

But at least I got that feelin' outta the way relatively early.

Despite the mental torture, my academic record didn't slip for the next three years of public school. Must've been that private school nurturing, or, so I'd like to think, some innate ability to do well in school. Maybe it was just the fear of fuckin' up, with my folks on my ass about my grades. Above-average report cards got me into the top class of each grade in junior high school. I didn't get lost in the tracking system that shuttles a lot of kids into sub-par expectations and low self worth. I couldn't understand how kids could be happy on report card day when they shouted, "Yes! All D's! I didn't fail anything!" Some kids timidly compared report cards with me, devouring mine with their eyes while keepin' mum on their own. I knew better than to ask.

Being "smart" in public school, naturally, led to being socially secluded to hangin' out with the rest of the geeks, brainiacs, and social misfits, thus being targets for the bruisers and ballers, the left-back warriors who had nothin' to lose,

8 L. R. WRIGHT
the ones who didn't care about suspensions and rebukes from lunch monitors and assistant principles. I learned to duck them well enough. Kept my mouth shut when someone rudely bumped my shoulder like I didn't exist, or when somebody took my spot on the handball court. I tried to speak up once, but when his big, three-years-older-than-me-muscle-head ass looked at me like I had the audacity to say somethin', I immediately cowered.

'You got it, man. You got it.'

'I know I got it, punk!'

I was an outcaste from the jump in public school, always out of the loop. I had to wear uniforms in private school, so I was always late on the fashions. My folks were, now that I think about it, rightfully reluctant to shell out big bucks for prime-time items. But that didn't matter to me at the time. If I was gonna be down with the nerd herd, I at least wanted to look good, right down to the fake Gazelle glasses and name belt buckle. Pops moaned and groaned about buyin' those white, shell-toed Adidas, all the way 'til he saw the shine on my face when I put the fat laces in'em. He didn't like buyin' expensive Jordache jeans from Delancy Street; the ones I never wore because I found out they were actually made for girls.

Moms wasn't too thrilled about my absolute need for every color LeTigre shirt, every color windbreaker, and every Lee color twill jean, including the pinstriped ones. I wore those bad boys out until the day I tried to pick on this girl Deanne, who kindly reminded me (think Tears for Fears), "Shout...shout..., Lee's are played out!"

I tried to fit in as best I could but somehow still stood out. For some reason, this one high school kid who I passed every morning walking to school during ninth grade would bump me, intimidate me, and look at me like, 'Yeah, what?' Dudes would practically dare me to look at them, only to demand "What the fuck you lookin' at" when I did. A few girls, mad 'cuz they caught me starin' at their hyper-developed booties, tried to get their boyfriends after me. I was lucky to have a friend who was a fellow brainiac but who also happened to be the one guy in school even the warriors wouldn't fuck with. By association, I escaped many an ass-whuppin'.

So, things weren't as bad as they could've been. I never got punched in the eye over some Zulu Nation beads. I never suffered the embarrassment of having my Lee jeans patch snatched from my ass. I never got slammed over a car for my sheepskin coat, like this poor, bloodied chap I once saw. I did get jumped once for my black suede Pumas, but the truants didn't hurt me, and some gentlemen walking his daughter home from school got'em back for me 'cuz I was too embarrassed to walk around with just socks on my feet.

Besides Moms, I didn't tell anybody about that back then, especially Pops. He would always tell me stories about how much of a bad-ass he was; a 135-pound linebacker, three varsity-star stud who'd have to run away after ball games 'cuz he didn't want his girlfriends charging the field to greet him and find out about each other. He was the first person his friends went to when some shit was goin' down.

I was just 135 pounds.

I never faced any real danger going to school in the Bronx, but I've seen some fucked up shit happen. Nowadays, city schools seem relatively safer compared to the potential disaster of young, white suburban angst. But back then, there were worse stories of going to school in the city, and I'm glad to announce that none of them happened to me. But as much as I wanted to be down, to be the bad ass Pops claimed to be, I wasn't. I was a straight-up outcaste, a "smart" student in public school. I collected GI Joe figures, comic books, and dreamed of bangin' the hottest honeys in school while the studs were doin' it.

I knew it would behoove me not to go to my zone school, Roosevelt, maybe still considered one of the worst schools in the city. I made several bids to enter specialized high schools like Herbert H. Lehman, Murray Bertram, Brooklyn Tech, and Bronx Science. But it was an attempt at a specialized educational program that ultimately decided what would happen with my education and my life.

A Better Chance was born during the height of the Civil Rights Era, one of the few concessions made by The Man to appease black protests for equality in education. White, upper class, New England educators came up with the idea of opening their private schools, with a few select scholarships, to impoverished black students who showed academic promise. ABC sprouted into a national not-for-profit organization funded by some federal money and grants, but mostly by private donors, and now includes all minorities.

Inner-city, minority applicants to the program take a test called the SSAT, a precursor to the SAT, are interviewed, and have their academic record evaluated. If accepted, the kid gets a scholarship to a prep school that participates in the program or lives in a boarding house with other ABC students and is bused to a public school in a wealthy town.

My first attempt at the program in eighth grade wasn't successful, but I got in when I applied in ninth grade, to begin going away in the tenth grade. I was disappointed that I didn't get accepted to a boarding school. Moms sent me away, a couple of summers before I got into the program, to summer school at Northfield Mount Hermon in Massachusetts, to see if I would be down for that kinda thing permanently. It was a blast. But for high school, I ended up going to a public school outside of Philadelphia and living the boarder-house life. Either way: the chance to go to a wealthy public school, to be away from home, away from hawking, parental eyes; the fact that I wouldn't have to worry about *if* I was going to college but rather *which one*; who in their right mind would pass up that opportunity? I know this sounds corny, but really, that's when I started to think that anything was possible.

I watched a lot of ill shit go down in NYC schools, from over-whelmed teachers to the fucked up tracking system, where once you're placed at a certain level, there's less possibility of hoping to excel to another, hence increasing the frustration of kids who wonder what the point of school is, hence killing any desire to learn, unknowingly making themselves better pod people for the architects of the games we play.

The idea had been firmly planted in my mind, ever since I could remember that education was the key to success in life. The only definition of success was being able to get a good job. With ABC providing me that opportunity, success was practically assumed. I began to ingest all kinds of platitudes; of "becoming somebody," of "being able to give something back" once I was "successful." Give what to whom wasn't quite clear, but by God, I'd be able to do it. But the real bottom line was that I'd be able to get a good job making lots of money if I accumulated as much education as possible. That was good enough reason for me to leave my home and walk through the door that ABC opened for me. The idea of education for learning's sake never entered my mind. It was all about the Benjamins, baby.

My folks were happy and excited that what they both wanted for me was happening. If buying all those toys and expensive, out-dated fashion was their way of bribing me to do well in school, it worked. I was to be the prodigal son, the one with the bright future. Pops joked that some day I'd buy him a forest-green Jaguar. I told him I would be glad to, even though he made me wear that damn green suit that one Easter. Knowing him better in retrospect than I could've back then, he showed nothing but smiles, but I know at some point he cried, even if it was just a little.

I was glad to be leaving New York, lookin' forward to a change in environment, to a future that seemed to hold so much promise. I had no fuckin' idea what I was getting into.

Alan: A Black Friend

"*I was very introverted as a child. I was geographically separated from my school friends. I had to figure out **how** to entertain myself. That's why even now I don't like a lot of people around **me all** the time. As an adult, people just bore me easily. I don't necessarily want to be around people unless they engage me.*

"*So I played a lot of video games. I had everything: Atari, Collecovision, Intellivision, Nintendo, and hand-**held** games. I had a lot of toys and stuff. Kids used to come over to my house. We had cable before anybody else did. We had a VCR before anybody else. I got into music a lot, too. I liked playing piano, but I wasn't disciplined enough [too get good], but I always played on my own, trying to figure notes out. I also read a lot more than your average kid: Superfudge, Hardy Boys, everything by J.D. Salinger.*

"*We lived in a gated community for the most part. We had a nice parking lot in the back. That was our playground. We used to play football, running bases: everything. It was cool in many ways because all our families moved into these townhouses when they were first built, so we were all relatively the same age. We had a group of about thirty kids who grew up together. It was our little society.*

"*So as with any society, you have your outsiders who aren't part of the society. I remember the first time I was even aware of the projects was when other black kids came through our neighborhood. They were 'bad' outsiders, the foreigners. I heard them referred to as shines, niggers, all kinds of racial epithets, but I had no idea what these words really meant. I had Filipino friends, white friends... I didn't know any better. I had no idea what that was all about. Race was never an issue in my childhood until I was around nine or ten years old, when this phenomenon was occurring in my neighborhood.*

"*I wound up sitting at the dinner table one night with my sister and my parents. I said, 'I don't know what's going on with our neighborhood here, Ma. It's a problem. All these niggers keep coming through our neighborhood.'*

"*I had no idea what the word nigger meant AT ALL! I'll never forget that awkward look I got from my parents. They didn't look at me, they looked at each other like, 'You're gonna be the one to handle this. He's YOUR son. You deal with this.' My mother finally cut in. She said, 'You know son, I hate to break it to you, but, you're a 'nigger.' You realize that, right?'*

"*So we had a long talk after that. I don't remember what was said to me, but first they told me that we're all black, and we're all one race, and nigger is a very bad word, and I shouldn't use that word. I still didn't quite understand it all at the time. That was the first time I experienced what racism was, I suppose.*

"*These other kids were obviously very proficient in it. They got it from their parents. There were a few other black kids in the community. I hung out with everybody, but I still didn't really think of us as 'black.' They weren't around during the 'nigger' and 'shine' discussions, I guess.*

"*It didn't help that I went to private school 1ˢᵗ through 12ᵗʰ grade. This was one of the top schools in the city, if not the best. Very few black people went there, as you can imagine. It always seemed to be, if you're black, you were from the*

South Side. A lot of [black] kids lived in Hyde Park (an affluent black community), and a few lived further into the South Side. White kids could walk to school. It was like a whole community there. A lot of kids went through high school, and some even in college, never having gone on the subway. I still think to this day that there are plenty of people from my high school that never stepped foot on a subway. I had to take a subway and a bus every day.

"Taking the train and the bus was a daily reminder that I wasn't a part of that community. I guess I always dreamed of living in one of those posh, high rise apartments that they lived in, with a doorman, where you just felt prestige as soon as you walked in. They're completely impractical because they're no bigger than my apartment most of the time, but they were just so nice.

"I was too young to be like, 'God, those kids are sheltered, and I'm glad that I have these life experiences and those kids don't.' I was too young to think about it. I thought there was something wrong with me because I had to hang out, on the bus and train, with the dregs of humanity, while these kids were skipping home to their little nice, high rise apartments on Lake Shore Drive. At the time, I was a snob just like everybody else at my school, maybe even more so, just because I was trying to over-compensate for not fitting in.

"I was always trying to fit in when I was in private school. It was a horrible place to be a minority. From as far back as fourth or fifth grade, I can remember developing a strong sense of humor at an early age. I was always the class clown. That was my way of gaining attention. Then it grew beyond that into this ability to empathize with people. I was really good at it. By sixth grade, I became the most popular kid in school. This was sort of a weird turn because I was so good at empathizing with people that at any given time, I could be talking to them and they would think that I was their best friend because I was so in touch with what they were going through. I myself wanted so badly to be liked that I somehow developed this ability to immediately get in touch with people. So I was popular in sixth grade for that reason.

"But then as everybody's hormones picked up and people were going through puberty and developing that sense of, 'Oh, that guy's cute' and all that stuff, I was cast further to the side. For some reason... and I can't put a finger on it, but I never, at any point, felt attractive. I don't know if it was because my dad taught me so, or because I genuinely didn't feel it. He almost made it a point to make it very clear that my peers would never accept me.

"'These white people will always smile in your face but always diss you behind your back. You should always be weary of them. I don't want you getting to close to them because I don't want you to be hurt someday when you figure this out.'

"I heard this time and time again. It was so painful as a child to listen to your father tell you on a regular basis that your friends are going to betray you and that he knew white people better than I'd ever understand them. He went to college and graduated with them, and he knew how deceitful they could be, and I was never going to be accepted, and I didn't quite understand it at the time because I hadn't hit puberty, but those white girls weren't gonna like me. They were not gonna go after me. And it was FUCKED UP!

"Even to this day, it's hard for me to accept the fact that someone is attracted

to me because, as a child, I was taught that I was never attractive. I thought, from an aesthetic point of view, I was attractive. I'd look in the mirror and think, 'Yeah, I'm happy with myself.' But I just knew no matter how aesthetically pleasing I may have been, it was never going to be seen as acceptable to other people, black or white.

"Certainly, none of the private school white women liked black men. There was no taboo set up then. It wasn't until I got to college that I realized that there was this taboo about white women liking black men. In my school, that certainly didn't happen. These Jewish people...their kids were well trained that there was no way in hell they would be going out with a black person, for one thing. Secondly, it just wasn't attractive. There were so few black people there.

"To exasperate things further, I remember I had this incident that happened to me around ninth grade, when kids started to do drugs and stuff. They assumed that I was a narc because I was so 'in' with everybody. Somehow, someone started spreading that rumor about me, that I was narc-ing people out to the authorities. So it totally made me feel self-conscious, and I was chastised from a lot of groups because of it.

"My school was a fucked up place to be in. It really was. I think a lot of black people that came through there are really fucked up. I have this one friend who is totally fucked up. She could never find herself; transferred from three different schools, now having these adjustment problems, can't find a career... I can't make the direct association, but my school had a way of infringing on your self-esteem. There were a few people that did it, but interestingly enough, they were always gifted. The self-assured black people that came out of there were always very talented. One of them grew up in my neighborhood. His father and my father are very close associates, so I grew up with him. He was very smart, went to get a law degree and a business degree. He never had a problem, seemingly, with my school. Likewise, this other kid who was in my class was at a genius kind of level. He went to Stanford and went on to work for NASA. He never seemed to have a problem either. I guess the logical explanation would be that these kids were so gifted that that was their self-assurance. Everybody acknowledged them as being incredibly gifted, so they always felt, if not as good, better than most kids, regardless of whether they were black or white. They were just on a different level.

"The rest of us seemed to be fucked in the head, never feeling good enough, never feeling attractive enough, and always having these crushes on white boys and girls who never seemed to like us back. Unrequited love was the norm for us. It kinda wears on you. I think the effects can be far more damaging at times than if someone was to just call you a nigger. You always heard about somebody making some nigger crack or something like that, but nothing major. I thought covert racism was a lot more painful and demoralizing in the end.

"I gave a Martin Luther King Jr. speech one time about that. This was the sort of thing where you're either in or you're out. I don't even know how to analyze this now, but I remember a lot of the frustration growing up in a school like mine had to do with ignorance. People weren't outwardly racist. It wasn't that kind of school. There was definitely difference established. You just didn't feel attractive to people. You were always just a friend: a black friend.

"*But people would ask stupid questions about your hair. 'Do you comb your hair? Do black people get sunburn?' Stupid shit like that. I heard these questions growing up, so I decided one time to do, for my Martin Luther King, Jr. speech, a forum of questions. I made up this mock situation. I wrote questions out. It was kinda funny, actually, at least at the time. I gave the questions to various members of the audience and had them ask the questions. I was like, 'You know, there's been a lot of questions abounding about black people versus white people, so I'm gonna open up the floor to a question and answer session.' So people asked the questions.*

"*'Alan, do black people comb their hair?'*

"*I'd say a funny anecdote. 'People think black folks don't have to comb their hair, but if we didn't, you'd see us comin' to school lookin' like Buckwheat.'*

"*It was unexpected. It took a while before people realized this was staged. I had these outrageous answers, and people would be like, 'Oh shit, this is kinda weird.' But then after a while, they realized that it was a game, so it became funnier. At the end, I thought it was really successful. Everybody was laughing, but I turned it around. I was like, 'Well, you know, I did this exercise to show that there's such a thing as covert racism, and people have prejudices. There are things that I've experienced that have not been so funny and so light-hearted.'*

"*There was a story. I told them about this locker incident I had. It was such a subtle thing. It had been sitting on my locker for a long time and I never saw it. Someone scratched 'Die Nigger,' but it was really small writing. A black friend pointed it out to me. He said, 'What the fuck is that on your locker?' That was really the only example of overt racism. I explained how that was a traumatic experience at the time, my junior year. The speech was moving at the end because it was a heartfelt speech.*

"*The black community was really upset by it. They were upset that I did the whole question and answer thing. They thought I was making light of issues that didn't need to me made light of, like making Buckwheat jokes. They thought it was forwarding stereotypes rather than diminishing them. I guess I could see the point they made, but it's like the argument that Keenan Ivory Wayans has with black folks all the time, when he stretches a joke too far. It's his way of dealing with the plight of black Americans, by making light of situations in hopes of forging dialogue, or whatever. Whatever it was at the time, I remember feeling very heartbroken because the last thing I wanted to do was offend black folks. I was sort of labeled a sellout at that point.*

"*But I had a few close [white] friends. There was no real clique, I suppose. All my friends were really smart. That was one thing we all had in common, for the most part. I just wound up hookin' up with them. A lot of the reason I made it to college, I guess, had to do with them because I was hanging out with such smart individuals. I always felt the need to keep up with them, which is fucking impossible, because still to this day they're some of the brightest individuals I know.*

"*We were always in honors classes together. We had this weird group of friends that were kinda considered nerds in a sense. Everybody sorta played his or her own games, admiring us from afar, but didn't want to be caught admiring us. It's a typical high school in the sense that everybody's tryin' to hang out with the beautiful people, but it's still a private school. There's a high premium placed on making it to a great college, an Ivy League school. You have to be into your studies to do that. Beyond being a jerk or being cool, there's an understanding that you gotta be good at schoolwork. So they may have thought we were nerds, but at the very same time, they admired us.*

"It's funny, when we graduated...it's really funny. Every time I run into people who were the cool kids, there's this respect that I always get from them. They almost feel guilty that they alienated us. It's like they wanted to hang out with us but just couldn't do it. Now, there's this mutual respect."

"I was on the basketball team up until sophomore year, but I was also acting. The two started to conflict until it got to a point where my coach was like, 'You're a phenomenal actor. As much as I want to see you play basketball, you should go ahead and do the acting thing full time.' It got ridiculous.

"That was my big high school thing. That was my claim to fame. I started acting when I was in eighth grade. It got a little more serious freshman and sophomore year. By sophomore year, I was starring in school plays. Junior year, I was THE star. There was this other kid, John Moses. He's still acting now. We were the marquis players. He was a year ahead of me, so by the time he graduated I was the star as a senior.

"I did a few plays. 'Master Harold and the Boys' is the one that people there always remember me for. It's about a South African household. Matthew Broderick played the original movie role. He was a white kid from the aristocracy. He had these two black servants. One was older, played by myself. He grew up with them. He was at the point where he was coming of age. Becoming a man, he knew that he could no longer view his servants as his friends. He had to act as if they were his servants. The whole play is about him going through this transition. Finally, in the last scene, he has a choice. He could either be a racist like his father, or he can defy all that. He decides that it's easier to be a racist, so he spits in the face of one of his servants...me.

"That's actin' fo' yo' ass, when you have someone spit in your face and you can't do shit about it. He spits, and it trickles down my face. I can't wipe it off for a minute and a half or so. Imagine rehearsal after rehearsal. First we pretend. By dress rehearsal, he's spitting in my face every time because we have to make sure it's right.

"School plays are usually considered to be a drag and something you had to go to. We were always the underdog, as with any school. They're always throwing more money into athletics than into theatre programs. We managed, with very limited funds, to do phenomenal things. I was part of a legacy of actors performing incredibly under limited resources. But still, people looked down on theatre.

"This was the only time that they showed the whole play during school assembly. Usually, what they would do, they'd show you an excerpt from a scene. But this time I guess they thought it was such a compelling piece of work that they showed it from beginning to end. There was a standing ovation. The only time, as far as I know, a school play has ever received a standing ovation [at my school].

"On one of the nights, I got approached by an agent who wanted to represent

me. So from that point I went on to do a few commercials, developing a nice little career for myself as a young actor, a young black actor. I did my first commercial when I was fifteen or sixteen. That was my forte. When I was interviewing for college, I think they just accepted me because of my theatre background and various other things. I didn't have the best GPA, my SATs were average, but I was a shining actor, and I was black, so of course I think that played into it.

"My father always hated my acting. He always wanted me to be a professional. He wasn't spending all this money for me to go to private school to be some actor. I could've gone to any public school for that, so he hated it from the beginning. He had an agenda for me and my sister. We had to go to private school for twelve years. That's eight thousand every fucking year. He was not fostering his child under these kinds of prices for him to be an actor, so it was a constant source of annoyance.

"I had a chance to go to Cherub's, this summer program at Northwestern University. It was very noteworthy. In fact, the summer I wanted to go, my friend Matt went, and Noah Wyle from 'ER' was there that summer. It's really prestigious. People who go to this program always end up being some sort of talent, either in plays, because Chicago's a big theatre town, or in the movies, or whatever. Dad didn't want to support it, was like, 'I'm not having my son as an actor. You're not doing this.'

"So that summer, I wound up having to go to Steppenwolf, which is a big theatre in town, and supported myself. I had to pay for it out of pocket because my dad would not pay for any acting pursuit. There was also Second City, which I did for three years. I had to pay for that, too. They had a high school troupe. We traveled around to different high schools and stuff. Second City was awesome. It was probably one of the best educations I received ever. I started as a sophomore and did it through senior year. Chris Farley was on the main stage when I was taking the high school classes, so we used to watch him all the time.

"I had this amazing background in theatre. I could have gone on to do a lot of shit. I guess I just listened to my father too much. I listened to the doubt in me that said, 'Black men will never be able to get a break in Hollywood. I'm not gonna prostitute my art and myself and just be in a state of misery for the rest of my life. I've got these other talents besides acting.'

"Here's an example of what I'm talking about. I hate to think cynically like this, but there's this guy I see all the time. He was on 'ER' for a while. He was also on one of those WB shows. He's always playing some nerd or something like that. I remember when I was a senior in high school, my acting theatre took us to see this play called 'The Meeting' at the Goodman Theatre, which is big in town. It was about the meeting of Malcolm X and Martin Luther King, Jr. He was in it as Malcolm X. PHENOMENAL! This guy was great. He over-shadowed the Martin Luther King guy by a long shot. Just incredible. Afterwards, I told him that that was an incredible performance.

"Since then; that was about nine, ten years ago; I don't see him in anything. I don't know what kind of aspirations he had. Maybe he toured the theatre circuit, because a lot of people prefer to do that rather than the big screen. I see him in bit parts here and there, fucking WB network or something like that. It really breaks

my heart to see such talented people like that having their genius exploited regularly by Hollywood. That's the kind of thing that made me decide that I could never act for a living. Whether that was a legitimate reason or not, I just knew there was no way I could do that. I'd rather go on to do something else.

"I'm pretty glad I made that decision. I just couldn't take that lifestyle of being a struggling actor. I just couldn't be waiting around for my agent to call me while I'm waiting tables. Some part of me kinda yearns for having a nine to five because I need that stability. Obviously, I'd love to be famous. That would be a dream to me. But again, realistically speaking, one out of a thousand people actually make it, white or black. If you add being black to the mix, your odds decrease. That's a pipe dream, literally. I couldn't do it.

"Honestly speaking, I don't regret it. But I sorta wonder, hell, what if I did it? It's not enough to make me want to get up and leave my job, but whose to say? Maybe I'm lying to myself, and I'll be 40 and have a mid-life crises, like, 'Damn, I want to be an actor!'

"But back then, I figured, 'I do have these other talents, and I have gone to the best school in the city, so I guess it's easier and more practical for me to go on and pursue something like pre-law,' which is exactly what I did."

The Grouch

I was affectionately known as "The Grouch" by some of the other ABC kids. I don't know specifically why, other than the fact that I snapped at people, always seemed to find something wrong with everything, and got angrier the nicer they were with me. I couldn't articulate why I was so grouchy all the time.

On the surface, I really had few reasons to be grouchy. I was probably luckier than most fifteen-year-olds. I was away from home, living in a house with 10 other boys and girls who were more than happy to engage in water fights, pillow fights, late-night basketball, and after-hours bullshit sessions. Basically, it was like going to your friend's house for a sleepover, only it was every night. It was fun. Waking up and going to school was the nuisance in between.

Livin' away from home had a way of making me feel grown and independent in the middle of relative luxury. Radnor is one of the wealthier suburbs of Philadelphia along Route 30 know as "The Main Line," approximately thirty to forty minutes outside the city. It didn't feel like going to high school as much as it did a small college. The spacious environment with manicured lawns invited the possibility of actually getting something out of school. It was surrounded by two baseball fields, a softball field, a soccer and lacrosse field, a field hockey field; sports that I didn't even know existed; and a football field. Inside were two gymnasiums and an Olympic-size swimming pool.

I've stepped into New York City public high schools only a few times, but enough to make a contrast and comparison. There is no comparison. The image of old, dirty, scratched, opaque, gated windows with murky sunlight coming through seems to dominate the feeling you get when you walk down the halls of a NYC public school. They look more like prisons, holdovers from the industrial age.

In Radnor, for grades nine through twelve, there were about 1,100 students and a full-time staff of about 100 professionals, most with advanced degrees. Roughly, that was a ratio of about 1 staff member to 11 students. Classes were small and the level of instruction commended a Department of Education award in 1984 by Ronald Reagan. How fitting.

No over-crowded classrooms, no shortage of materials or resources; an all-around pleasant environment to be in. I didn't have to walk to school wonderin' if that day was gonna be the day that I wouldn't squeeze out of an ass-whuppin' (This was before you had to worry about white boys with grudges and automatic weapons). There were few barriers to productivity. Most everyone encouraged learning. You were a geek by looks and actions mostly, not mainly because you had a high GPA.

On top of all this, we in the ABC house were even more pampered than some of the kids who actually lived in the community. We lived under the care of a resident director and his family. He was an ABC alumnus, he related to us well, and he knew how much rope to give us. There were also three live-in tutors who monitored two and a half-hour study sessions Sunday through Thursday. They helped us with homework, papers, SAT preparation, college applications, and one of them schooled us on the finer points of adult entertainment. The level of assistance was incredible.

The one thing they couldn't help us with was how to deal with being in, for most of us, a completely alien environment. Radnor Township, back then, was home to about 30,000 whites, although the ABC brochure tried to make us feel better by informing us of the "well integrated low-income areas," in case we got too homesick. I traded the relative diversity of the Bronx for the lily-whiteness of Radnor. In the Bronx, I was barely conscious of race matters. It wasn't so much about race as it was about culture. White, black, Hispanic, and Asian kids from around the way all wanted to be down in the days of Run DMC, pop-lockin', break dancing, and shell-toed Adidas. When I got to Radnor, everything turned black and white. Part of it had to do with the ABC program itself. Whatever our ethnicity, it became a stamp: "bright, promising black students, or Hispanic students, or Asian students." Tag, you're it.

As people of color in an environment like Radnor, we weren't just who we were. In the minds of the town folks, and even some of the volunteers of the program, we were a walking set of assumptions, a living projection of the stereotypes that have always plagued minorities. The thing is; nobody was trying to be racist. To a lot of people, minorities who come from the city must be charity cases. Before we even had a chance to show ourselves, we were already tagged by the Radnorites, most of them having had little or no contact with ordinary black or brown folks.

Even though I felt like an oddball at times in the Bronx, just like any adolescent feels in any situation, there was at least some level of social stability. When I got to an environment where very few people looked, talked, and dressed the way I did, things got really fucking complicated. It was a field of opposites, the inevitable, internal tug of war because of being black in a "white" environment. There was the one side that virtually said, "Welcome to our world. You are here because you have been deemed worthy of a chance. You have more potential than others, so you deserve an opportunity to fulfill that potential. Here's how we do things."

Then there was the other side that said, "Congratulations. You're getting a chance many of us don't get. Work hard, don't let'em get you down, we wish you well. But remember who you are and where you come from. You may find 'them' to be racist, calling you names, treating you bad, but you don't have to like them and they don't have to like you. Just remember why you're there." That was code for "Don't sell out!"

That's always been a funny thing to me, this whole notion of selling out. What exactly is "selling out" for a black person? Tryin' to be "white?" How does one *be* black or white?

Hmmm. I'm surrounded by white people. I'm supposed to adjust myself in order to learn how to play The Game, but I'm not supposed to imitate them. I'm supposed to play by the rules to get what I need. I'm not supposed to get too close, *especially* with the women, that unwritten, ominous taboo. Oh. Okay.

That's where it started for me, the whole absurd set of contradictions of what it's supposed to mean to be black in America. In many ways, we do imitate, but we're not supposed to assimilate, the black politically-correct response to this society's enduring resistance to acknowledge the apartheid-like history of this country, and its enduring effects, that make true assimilation impossible anyway. Then again, the only way to live and survive in this country is "The American

Way," so we've got no choice but to try and participate, right? It requires assimilation to a certain degree, but then there's that old barrier of our skin and the perceptions that have been built into it, creating what W.E.B. Dubois called the "double consciousness" inherent in all black people: being "black," which, historically in America, meant being delegated to a less-than-human status, yet being American at the same time, an identity that was originally equated with being "white." Black people live with the tension of wanting inclusion despite our frustration of America's resistance to inclusiveness, whether that resistance is a result of choice on the part of society at large, or the inevitability of historical effect.

There's a part of all black people that wants to "sell out" in the sense of wanting acceptance and acknowledgement of our humanity. On the other hand, there's a quiet acceptance that perhaps things will never change, and the best we can hope for is the 21st century version of separate but equal, not legally separated from society at large, but separated because of the de facto results of government-sanctioned segregation. That frustration, that resentment, is what creates the notion of not "selling out" to white folks; a mindset of choosing to stay separated because it's inevitable anyway.

There was never a clear definition, to me, of what it was to sell out. Nobody ever actually told me, "Don't sell out," but I responded to that thing: that thing, which growing up in America, we all respond to, that thing we can't see or touch, but we know it's there, and we know it has rules, just as sure as we know the sky is blue. It's the thing that separates us into "others," with jaded perceptions and implicit directions to stay separated, and the result is that we're not able to break through to each other's humanity, hence denying our own without being aware of it. We are more than socially-designated colors.

I didn't know what to expect goin' into Radnor. I had no expectations, fantasies, or fears. I just knew I was gonna stand out. Race was front and center in my consciousness. It was the first time I felt like a "minority." It was like being on a stage, acting out an expected, acceptable role. Since I thought this was the case, I had to come correct and make sure that I was representing minorities. I went in with a mentality like, "Fuck this, I'm not gonna let white people change me. I don't care what these people think." My number one concern, outside of doing well in school, was to make sure that I didn't forget where I came from.

So I started out dressing like my interpretation of a Bronx B-Boy; one pant leg rolled up, a gold chain and gold plate with my initial on it, fresh Nikes, and, when weather permitted, a leather bomber jacket that I begged poor Pops to buy me. I wouldn't have dared to wear any of that shit in the Bronx, shit that I've seen kids get slammed over cars for. But in Radnor, I tried to personify the Bronx.

The Beastie Boys had just made hip-hop more palatable to 'burbanites, so I thought I was part of a vibe, the living persona of what white people thought of a hip-hop B-Boy. I bopped down the hallways and punctuated my slang. I was just being ridiculous; really, I was living up to an image of what I thought white people would expect to see. I was playin' them and myself. Or maybe just myself.

I cringe at how badly I was tryin' to be "black" in the white environment. One day a white guy in my French told me that I looked like a pimp. I was too square back then to take that as a compliment, but his observation nonetheless snapped me out of that role-playing. Eventually, I traded that ridiculousness for another: Gap sweaters and khakis, cuffed at the ankle, and Eastland loafers, back when only white people shopped at The Gap. The things a brotha will do for acceptance.

It took a little while, but eventually us ABC kids settled into as much comfort as we were gonna get given the situation. None of us were in any threat of forgetting who we were. How the hell can you forget when you're the constant object of nervous glares, curious stares, and second glances? Some people didn't even acknowledge our existence or didn't know how to deal with the fact that they didn't know how to deal with people that were different than them. Sometimes it was easier for them to just ignore us.

But it wasn't all bad. As with any place, there were a few people willing to reach out and make a connection, even if it was primarily to satisfy their curiosities. I was always so damned innocent and believing in the best of people. I took it for granted that I could get along with anybody. Whoever wanted to be my friend could, until the umpteenth time I got asked something stupid, like, "Does the ABC program buy clothes for you guys?"

"No, motherfucka! We're not homeless! Jeez!"

I had to learn not to take offense, though. Whatever pressure there was for me to "keep it real," I made friends. What the hell else does a teenager want but comfort in a social situation? A large part of our identity gets shaped through other people's eyes. And so began the split into the unknown for me, like an amoebae breaking away from the parent. The shaping of an identity got blurred and unfocused, with two seemingly opposite points of view: black and white. I knew I was black. I was reminded of it every day, but because I was spending those all-important pubescent years around whites, I couldn't help but incorporate that into my make-up. I changed. It's an inescapable part of what it means for people of color to develop in predominantly white environments. Only the degree of change is relevant. All too often, the more we change, the more we run the risk of being labeled a sellout.

Thankfully, I never had to deal with being called that. Not to my face, anyway. It was more like a feeling, a feeling of not belonging. Nobody had to do or say anything to me, but I still felt it, like when I was around black folks and I'd slip and say, "EEEE-ZEEEE," when I should've said, "Nigga Pleez!" Or when I was thoughtlessly mumblin' Van Halen lyrics and I got that "Nigga, what's wrong with you" look.

It was a funky paradox. I was doin' all I could to prove to white folks that I knew who I was and that I had no intention on sellin' out to them, whatever that meant. But when I was around people I should've been able to identity with, or rather, felt compelled to identify with, I felt anxious to not act "white" for fear of dealing with comments like, "That's white-boy music." "That's the way white people dress."

It's a fucked up thing to be shunned by your peeps at home, a place where you're lookin' to feel comfortable and at ease after being the object of curiosity in lily-white land. But that's the hardcore reality of traveling between two worlds. It was like I became two people, shifting between both worlds but not really belonging to either. To shun one meant cutting off potential for upward mobility. To shun the other meant giving up a part of who I was before the opportunity arrived, and to feel the animosity of those who felt left behind.

Of course, these weren't things I consciously thought about back then. I made the best of what I had, with a constant nagging in the back of my head about the awkwardness of the situation. At this point, there was only a vague, faded outline of a question mark forming in my mind.

If I was ever tryin' to make some kind of social stand against the rich white kids in the Alpha clique, it worked. Through those unknown twists of high school fate, I ended up befriending those who were deemed the school losers. I hate sayin' that, but...fuck it, they *were* the school losers. But they accepted me; they kept their "Do Black people..." questions to a minimum, and I had people to sit with in the small cafeteria where all the other assorted nerds, geeks, losers, and other invisible high school kids sat. The beautiful people: the athletes, studs, cheerleaders, and otherwise popular people sat in the main cafeteria.

The only reason I ever had to go to that cafeteria was to collect my free lunch, a benefit of bein' a poor, under-privileged minority. The embarrassment of the daily ritual was minimized by the fact that the watered-down orange drink didn't come with the lunch, so I could save *some* pride by pullin' money out of my pocket every time I went to get lunch. But the lady had to mark me off her list, so the game was still given away.

There were a few kids I met in the small cafeteria that were actually quite nice, capable of giving respect, quietly acknowledging our differences but not basing a relationship on those differences. That was a rarity. No matter what their status, when I found people like that, I called them friend.

My best friend from town moved away our senior year. The ABC kids always stuck together, but we still had to have our own lives and our own friends. So what clique do I end up in? Guys with nicknames like "Booger" and "Pilot," two reasons why I really grew to appreciate "Beavis and Butthead." I was friends with this guy Mike by association, two outsiders delegated to lunch in the small cafeteria and the library during free periods, reading old issues of Rolling Stone magazine. Mike was friends with Booger and Pilot, so that made us a clique. Booger was Aryan all the way with short-cropped, stark blond hair, blue eyes, and a pigeon-toed, stormtrooper stomp. It astounded me how stupid he acted outside of the classroom, but once he was inside, he was smart, arrogant, and bull-shitted as well as anybody. Pilot wasn't too bright and exaggerated this to make Booger think he was cool for not giving a fuck. He always did this thing where he swooshed the hair down behind his left ear every time he said, "Yeeeaaaasssss." Mike was tall and kinda goofy, a bench-warmer on the soccer team and very restricted by his parents.

At first, it was cool. It was through Pilot that I first heard about N.W.A., as he snickered that it stood for "Niggas With Attitude." We had, hands down, the best homemade costumes for Senior Dress-up Day as KISS. I was the Cat-dude. We gave each other shot outs in the yearbook. We went to Booger's hockey games.

I also ignored a lot of shit, though, like the fact that Booger was anti-Semitic. "Fucking Jews" this and "Goddamn Yids" that, for no reason at all. I suspect he got it from his father. Pilot, who really wasn't anti-anyone, followed Booger's cues. The thought occurred to me that maybe they were sayin' all kinds of shit behind my back, but I didn't believe that they really believed what they were saying. It just sounded cool and funny, to them, to use slurs. But who knows? Maybe I was just kiddin' myself for the comfort of having "friends," and they're somewhere in Idaho right now, paranoid, training for the coming racial apocalypse.

Hangin' out with them wasn't the problem, besides the occasional "Hey Ron, you sit in the back" car jokes. It was their other friends that pissed me off. The extent to which they didn't think twice about their ignorance confirmed something I began to suspect: that people of color are totally invisible to a lot of whites. We might as well be walking shadows. It also had to do with them thinking, "Well, Ron's not *really* black. He's smart and he likes rock music." The most interesting thing about the situation was that I actually got to see how casually they tossed insults around.

A typical case was when I was ridin' around in a car with three white boys: Hank and Carmen, the Marchesani twins, and this loser Stan. The Marchesanis were cool, but a little on the impatient tip (Hey, they were Italian. Whaddaya gonna do?). We were stopped at a light, waiting for it to turn green. As the light turns, a black guy walks in front of the car. Hank yells, "Yo asshole, get the fuck outta the way!" Not enough, Stan yells, "Yeah, nigger-spook!" From the backseat, I chirped, "Yeah Stan, that's real fuckin' funny."

"Oh, sorry Ron."

Another moment of awareness came at this guy Chris' house, another trashy idiot. Everybody loved Chris' dog, a black retriever. Chris, with me standing near, lovingly refers to him as his "coon-dog." I pretend not to hear while everybody tries to quietly shush him up.

But my favorite character was Nick, probably the biggest loser in the group. A constant whiner, consummate under-achiever, and otherwise not good at anything, Nick didn't know the meaning of the word "class."

"Duuuude, I saw this black rock group 'Living Color' at 'Nova this weekend. Dude, they suck. Throw 'em some turntables. They'd be better off."

"Duuuude, Hank and Carmen need to get rid of that fucking nigger car."

"Duuuude, I'm gonna get me some watermelon Slice today," while he glances and smirks at me.

Nick wouldn't think twice about sayin' stupid shit like that whether I was there or not. I'd seen him get his ass kicked by this other black dude, so obviously that approach wouldn't have changed anything. Besides, I wasn't confrontational anyway. If people are gonna be idiots, fuck it. I got that down relatively early.

I learned to ignore him, as well as all the blank staring, stupid questions, and other daily demeaning activity ABC kids endured. I tried not to be too angry about the situation or take it out on other people, but I was a grouch. I put on blinders and shut down my emotions. I couldn't afford to focus on emotion. My whole reason for being became shaped by the fact that I was in this program whose purpose was to open the door so I could elevate myself.

I developed a certain sense of selfishness. I began to think of the whole thing as a game. I studied, did fairly well in most of my classes, and a few times I got scores higher that what I deserved because certain teachers didn't *expect* me to do that great. But hey, it was part of the game. In my mind, only the score mattered, and most of the time I earned it anyway.

When it came to my relationships with teachers, "friends," other students, and even some of the ABC volunteers, it often felt like a game. Do what you gotta do to get what you need. Other considerations, like mental and emotional well being, fell by the wayside, not that I was conscious enough to think of such matters at that point anyway. It was all about the game. It was the best and only game in town. ABC was my agent, grooming me to be the best player I could be. And what I had to win was status and prestige, the fruits of education.

With some kind of future goal in mind, however elliptical, it became easier to endure being in that environment, because when I was sittin' in that office overlooking downtown Manhattan, finalizing the purchase of a forest-green Jaguar for Pops, it would've all been worth it. How? I didn't know. It was assumed as part of the package of the fruits of higher education. These Radnor folks got it. Why can't I?

One of the things that might surprise people about the situation is that I never, in my entire life, have been called anything racially demeaning to my face. I think one of the main reasons I came into Radnor the way I did was to scare off anybody who ever thought of callin' me a nigger. I was lucky, in a sense, never having had to deal with that kind of humiliation.

The thing that bothered me about being at Radnor was the feeling of not being "normal," like my moves and actions as an "other" were being studied. It seemed like every minute spent in school, and in the town itself, reminded me of my blackness. Yeah, it was paranoia, but I almost couldn't help it. I was always wonderin' what kind of fucked up notions the next person would have of me, always trying to anticipate and prepare for the next uncomfortable situation. My response to certain people became automatic and programmed, cutting off spontaneity and faith that maybe this next person wouldn't see me as a cardboard character, the smart black kid from the Bronx, the under-privileged ABC student who gets free lunch and has "dreams" of "being somebody," like the caption said under a picture of me, Alice and Anthony in the town weekly newspaper when they did a story on us. *'Oh honey, how cute. The little brown and black kids from New York have dreams.'*

As a person of color in a mostly white environment, I stood out enough as it was. I didn't want to do or say anything more than I had to, because when you're feeling uncomfortable, you don't want attention drawn to you. If you don't shine as an athlete, in academics, or some other talent, you're just a charity case, noticed but still somehow invisible. Before joining the program, I had vague notions about racism but hadn't yet appreciated its subtlety. I never gave thought to what being black meant, and because I still didn't know, it became somewhat of a pre-occupation. When it came to people I met, and in many situations, I read my blackness into it. *"Should I act niggerish, or should I speak articulately?"* Because of my insecurities, most everything became a reflection of imposed, sometimes self-imposed, definitions of blackness. Somewhere in the middle was a teenage kid tryin' to find some semblance of normality.

But how can you feel normal when everyday you're reminded of the fact that you're some kind of special case, the only person of color in history class that had to sweat through another lesson on Civil Rights? Sometimes even the teachers didn't realize how they could unintentionally embarrass us.

"Class, we're talking about a whole generation of people who marched, bled, died, had rocks thrown at their heads, dogs at their feet, and who endured terrific hardships for basic American rights. We still have a long way to go to true equality, but if you look around you today, you can see we have indeed come a long way. And I'm proud to say we have an example of that progress sitting right here in our classroom today..."

Fuuuuuck! Here we go. I've been deemed a spokesman for the race. Well, since we're on the topic...

"Ron, why don't other black people want to learn," this silly-ass blond named Heather asked. The sad thing is that I stammered out some kinda answer about lack of hope or something like that. I didn't know, at the time, to tell them about American history, the depth of the effects of slavery and segregation, and how that kinda tends to fuck up generations of people when sustained over hundreds of years. I didn't know to tell her that despite history, most of us are relatively okay.

After that class, a few kids, out of guilt or curiosity, would come up to me, pat me on the back, congratulate me for being smart (and black!), then maybe say hi to me in the hallways for the next couple of days. I told myself that I didn't want anything to do with most of those kids. I hated how self-assured they seemed, striding down the hallways confidently, happily engaged in their secure lives.

"Beth, are you going to Braaaad's party tonight?"

"Yaaaaah!"

"It's gonna be soooo aaaaawwwesome, ohmigod!"

Just like any high school kid, I felt the pull to be popular and liked, despite the fact that I didn't like any of them. My little 135-pound, skinny ass tried out for football. After two weeks and a hard helmet to the chest, I got flattened back to reality and the marching band, another notch on the geek belt, but I did graduate from cymbals to bass drum. That's progress, mo-tha-fuck-a!

I ran track 'cuz, hey, we're fast, aren't we? That and the fact that it guaranteed my one and only varsity letter on my spankin', shiny-red, nylon school jacket. I tried out for wrestling, losing what little weight I had and all three of my exhibition matches. I played lacrosse, and surprisingly, was pretty good, considering I had never heard of lacrosse before tenth grade. I got sick of that too by senior year, when my coach was more interested in using my speed than in my desire to develop into a better player. So I settled for after-school, intramural floor hockey, whereupon the coach asked me, *"You sure you know how to play this sport, son?"*

"Gee, I don't know, Gersty. Are you allowed to bounce the puck?"

Any teenager from a different environment is gonna have difficulty fittin' in. But the one thing I couldn't escape was the color of my skin and the assumptions that went along with it. It was nearly impossible to feel a sense of security and belonging. I always questioned how people saw me, in turn, questioning myself. It induced deep-seated discomfort and mistrust, and shook the foundation on my sense of self and my relationships with others.

Don't get me started on relationships. I had absolutely, positively, no romantic associations in high school. I took a few shots, though. Didn't waste any time, either. In the second month of my first year, there was Lynn, my first high school crush, a bouncy, stringy brown-haired JV cheerleader. She had this annoyingly attractive habit of gettin' up close to my face and batting her green eyes whenever we talked. I don't even know why I liked her so much, other than the fact that I thought she liked me. We sometimes took the school bus together to football games, whenever I didn't feel like ridin' with the band. She flirted. I gushed. My roommate, a senior, goaded me into asking her out, either because he sincerely thought I had a chance, or out of some perverse desire to see me get shot down. I wrote my first love letter, in history class, to her. After that class, I heard, "Oooh, I feel so bad, you're a nice guy, but..." for the first time. I didn't have the courage to ask somebody else out until senior prom.

I did have other chances, or rather, dim hopes. There was Kristen, who I had a strong suspicion liked me, and who I knew had a black boyfriend before, so that wouldn't have been an issue. But after the Lynn debacle, I wanted no part of further possible rejection. There was Angela, a big-bootied sista who wore too much make-up. We planned an after-school rendezvous to meet in the basement. I even got the gumption to buy condoms at the pharmacy, back when it was still embarrassing to do so. She never showed up. Then there was Michelle, a beautiful Jamaican girl who told me at lunchtime on my 16th birthday that she had something to give to me but couldn't give it to me in school. Lord Jesus, I don't remember why that never worked out. Slow on the trigger, probably.

Romance in high school – non-existent. Shit. No wonder they called me The Grouch. A small consolation was that I wasn't the only ABC guy, or girl, to go through that sort of thing.

Finding a date for the senior prom was an anxiety-filled feat. I had plenty of female friends, all with boyfriends. I asked this one acquaintance of mine, who didn't go to my school, but I got the message after the third time she said, "I'll call you back," and didn't. I even called Michelle, who graduated a year before me and sounded annoyed that I had the nerve to call her. Out of desperation, a few days before the prom, I flipped through the directory and got the number of one of the very, very few black girls in my class. Mind you, I might've said all of two words to her beforehand, but what the hell, "You're black and dateless, I'm black and dateless. Let's do this..." I didn't say that, but then again, I didn't have to. We parted ways before the night was over. The date was like an unspoken business deal. "We'll keep each other from feeling like total losers, and then when it's over, we'll politely go our separate ways." What happened to the whole sweetheart thing? What happened to clumsy fumbling, heavy breathing, and foggy car windows? What happened to the life-long friends, times you never want to forget? I still can't watch those 80s high school movies without feeling like I was cheated.

I couldn't wait to get away from high school. I told Moms once that I hated school, not really knowing why at the time. But she urged me to stick it out, and I did. She was filled with jubilation at my graduation, proud of her baby and what he accomplished, and the possibilities of what was to come. I feigned the same sentiments, cheering with a hole in me, like wind goin' through a tunnel. I plastered a smile on my face, took pictures, hugged people, and shook hands, but there was something missing. I was convincing myself that I was happy, forcing myself to be happy. I graduated high school, and I was going to college. I'd be out of that place, away from Radnor, away from the stigma of what it was to be an ABC student.

Academically, high school really wasn't that difficult. I had good training and did well enough to move on with relative ease. But it was ABC that opened that door of opportunity for me. Fine. I was ready to run through it and away from it, blindly into the future, with only a vague concept of why I was doing this, with visions of success, achievement, of "being somebody," and hopefully one day feeling "normal."

The hardest part of that time was when I got a phone call on April 7th, 1989, the year I graduated high school. I had just gotten back from visiting Hampton University in Virginia. It rained a lot that day. I thought I'd be excited by a visit to a black college after the whole Radnor debacle, but I wasn't. No matter where I was, that alien feelin' would follow me like a cumulous cloud.

That day, sitting in the lobby of the campus auditorium around 3 p.m., the time I was later to find out Pops passed away, I felt an exceptional sting of loneliness. The tour was over, the other visiting students went their separate ways, and I sat around, protected from the rain, waiting for several hours for the shuttle back to the airport, to catch the plane back to Philly.

Moms called earlier and left a message for me at the ABC house to call her back, no matter what the time. As soon as I heard her voice, I knew. All she said was, "We have to take care of your father. You know what I mean, right?"

I knew he had cancer a long time before that. Sometimes he did okay with it, living life relatively normally, and sometimes he was too weak to move. It seemed that he was off and on chemo, in and out of the hospital. I didn't really know the extent and seriousness of the disease, and they never wanted me to have the burden of knowing.

I was relatively calm about it. The previous three years of numbing myself must've helped a little bit. I don't know if my roommate Anthony was there that night on the bottom bunk, but I quietly climbed to the top, buried my face in the pillow, and choked on sobs.

Almost a week later, I was back at that church in St. Augustine, Florida. I tried my damndest not to cry, to be strong, the way I imagined Pops wanted me to be. I wanted to be strong for Moms, for all the aunts and uncles and cousins I loved seeing so much with him. But I couldn't help it. I cried uncontrollably, careful never to look Moms in the eye. This time I knew better. No smile would've been able to comfort me.

A couple of weeks after Pops' death, I got my acceptance letter from Georgetown University, the confirmation of all that he and Moms wanted – nevermind that, at that point, I wasn't too thrilled about the whole concept of school. I was beginning to have doubts about the usefulness of it all, but that thought barely found the light of day in my head. Acceptance to a big name school, vague concepts of a better life: there was no choice. There was only the assumption that this was the way to go.

Alan: More of an Individual

"Freshman year in college was my first avenue into learning about the 'black experience.' I was so hyped being a naïve little freshman. I joined this group called 'The Forum.' It was all black men and we read books on black topics. I can't remember any of them now. I mean, the only black book I read in high school was The Autobiography of Malcolm X during my senior year. By the time I was a freshman in college, I was really hungry for the black experience.

"Over a while, though... Me personally, I felt that if you weren't kind of an inner city black, you really didn't fit into the black community. And I don't really consider myself inner city because although I grew up in the city, I went to private school, so I didn't have that slang talk. I felt like you had to have a little bit of slang to you, a little 'street.' It was a weird thing because there were a lot of incredibly bright, studious black folk AND they were street savvy, which I lacked. Immediately I felt...I had never been acculturated into that. Even now, breakin' on people, like playin' the dozens, all that shit, is something I was never accustomed to. I'm sorta always on guard when I feel someone's ostracizing me because of that. I take it more personally than I should.

"Everybody had these Community Scholars (a small, pre-freshman year program attended mostly by minorities), and I didn't go to Minority Student Weekend when I was a senior in high school. I felt like all these black people knew each other. I was like, 'What the fuck happened without me?' Seriously, I was overwhelmed by the whole college experience in general the first week I was there. All I did was hang out in my dorm room. I couldn't wait to get out of class and go back to my room. I hated those little events because I'd be at them by myself. I had nobody to talk to. I went to the same school for twelve years. I knew everybody for twelve years; never had to make friends for twelve years, so going to a new campus where I had to introduce myself was so out of control. I couldn't deal with that.

"It's a godsend that we met the way we did at that big function. I befriended Rod in my dorm, and he knew a few other people, and we all met up at Decatur's. From that point on, it was blind luck that the Lord wanted us to meet each other. Regardless of whether or not I talk to those folks today, I shared a lot of good times with them in college. It was great that we got a chance to meet each other like that.

"We shared similar backgrounds. We'd gone to predominantly white schools and we understood. We just understood. There was a vibe that we felt having to be a minority all the time, and finally here we are amongst each other, all having been 'minorities,' and now being able to commiserate together. I felt an instant bond with these people. There was no need to be judgmental. At times, people in the clique were judgmental, but it was always in good fun versus, like, the basketball players and their immediate clique.

"They were very judgmental, I felt. There was no way I'd be able to hang out with them because they'd be instantly jumpin' on my shit, and I just couldn't have that. At the time, I was very defensive about that. Now, I'm like, 'Fuck you! You don't like me; you can kiss my ass. That's the way it is. There's no way in hell I'm gonna convince you that I'm 'black' enough. If you knew me, you may or may not

*determine that I'm black enough, but I'm damn sure not gonna sit here and be blue
in the face tryin' to teach you that.' I'm way over that, but at the time, I was very
insecure about it.*

*"That's why Rod and I were so close for so long. His school was very, very
preppy, as was mine. We just had a lot in common in that regard. It's blind luck
that he was two rooms down from me in the dorm. I don't know how the Lord
managed to fit us together in that way, but he was lookin' out for us.*

*"I was used to a certain environment in high school, so to some degree, I
liked goin' to certain venues in Georgetown, those cheesy bar/dance clubs like
Winston's. Sure, 'Soul Night' at the campus Pub had its place, but I definitely liked
the Winston's, Champion's crowd too. I liked hanging out with Rod specifically
because he appreciated that as well. We bonded more on those sorts of issues,
going out to 'mixed' clubs like The Dome, where on Thursday night you could
drink 25-cent beers. Goddamn, it was so different in college. I remember just bein'
on the dance floor, toungin' girls 'cuz, hey, we were in college.*

*"There was a certain freedom that came with my friends. Like when I brought
that Asian girl home that one night or something like that. I didn't have to worry
about motherfuckas talking shit about how I was with an Asian girl. They'd be like,
'Yo, good for you, you got your groove on.' I just didn't view shit like others. Honestly
speaking, I'm not tryin' to be like, 'I don't see color. I just see people.' That's
bullshit. But I'm much more comfortable crossing racial lines than other people
are.*

*"I didn't feel like I had to defend myself to any one of our friends. Anybody
else outside, they'd be like, 'Ah, look at this motherfucka.' I just don't wanna hear
that shit! That's so limiting. That just demonstrates close-mindedness. We're so
close-minded sometimes, and we're always talkin' about how white people are
prejudiced against us, when in many ways, we're MORE close-minded than THEY
are. Ugh, God! That's always been a big problem for me.*

*"Like that girl Terry. You remember her, black girl? I was so in love with her
freshman year. Loved that girl! I had a New Order poster up in my room. She was
like, 'Psssmmph. I been knowin' you for a while. What you got New Order on your
wall for?' I was like, 'I like their music. You know, 'Bizarre Love Triangle,' 'True
Faith?' I KNOW you liked that. You went to Groton private school, so I know they
were playin' it. Don't play like you don't like it!' She's like, 'Yeah, I know, but I
wouldn't be puttin' that shit on my wall.'*

*"That really hurt me. Terry was a country gal and she kinda fell closer to the
basketball clique. She went to Groton, so she sorta had that boarding school thing,
but still, her leanings were more toward her country upbringing. So in many ways,
she definitely attacked me a lot in terms of me being too 'assimilated.'*

*"But I definitely look back fondly on my memories of college. It teaches you
a lot about yourself. They always talk about this in psychology, about the four
stages black intellectuals go through. I think it's, first, you're totally immersed in
white academia. Then secondly, you reach a stage in college where you come into
contact with more and more black people. There's conflict, inside and outside of*

you. Next, you go through a black militant stage. Finally, you get to a point where you settle all these issues, incorporate them, and then come to true self-understanding.

"*I went through a lot of that. I was 'militant.' Reading the Malcolm X autobiography pushed me into Georgetown because I came with the full intention of being completely militant. I remember having the black-nationalist flag on my wall the first week I was there. I thought about joining a black fraternity sophomore year, junior year. That was me goin' through my phase of tryin' to get pro-black, back in touch. I'd been deprived of all this hangin' out around my own. I wanted to be part of something.*

"*It was a lot of glamour. A lot of it had to do with Spike Lee's 'School Daze.' I remember seeing that movie my senior year in high school, maybe my junior year. I had never even heard of what a fraternity was. I saw the paraphernalia my dad had, but I had no idea what being a black Greek was all about. It was very glamorous to me for some reason. Seeing black folks in college was a glamorous thing to me. That's how unexposed I was. I really didn't even know about black people going to college. That made me want to go to Howard University, and all this stuff, based purely on 'School Daze' for the most part, made me want to join a fraternity. I thought there was something oddly cool about having to go through all this shit for a long time, so you could earn some shit, and feel proud of some shit, and say that you did some shit. It wasn't even so much a social thing. That's the part of the whole fraternity thing that ended up disturbing me. I faintly realized that there were some perks that went along with it, like getting women. But I had no idea to what degree until I had long made the decision that I wasn't gonna do it. Then I saw the* [black Greek fraternity] *gettin' pussy left and right. But that was never why I wanted to do it.*

"*I thought the* [another black Greek fraternity] *were about shit, tryin' to do things for the community and tryin' to heighten awareness. Over time, I saw that they really didn't do that. By the time I was a junior, it seemed very phony and fake to me. I began to see how silly the whole thing was. I was looking at these brothas and sistas who were actually in fraternities and sororities. They just didn't seem cool to me.*

"*I couldn't imagine doing that... I mean, it would've been fun. There DEFINITELY would have been some perks. But now, I would hate to be obligated to go to all these fucking functions and have all these motherfuckas come through town, look up your name in some directory, then call you, and you HAVE to take them out. You HAVE to put them up in your house. I don't know this motherfucka from Jack. He's callin' me because he called the fraternity and said, 'Do you know any brothas in Chicago?' I just could not fucking do that shit.*

"'*So yo, where da' ho's at?'*

"*I'm responsible for these stupid clowns from the University of Tennessee? I gotta entertain their asses? Oh God, I would just fucking hate that.*

"*I don't remember specifically why I didn't go through with trying to pledge. I think I was going to be the only one or something like that, or they weren't gonna have a pledge line. Maybe I was busy, had a play. For some reason or another, from a logistics standpoint, I couldn't do it. I thought it was bullshit, anyway. I became more of an individual, and I'm glad."*

"*I just know it was very difficult to feel at ease because there were so many rumors amongst the black community. It's natural, when you have any small community like that that sections themselves off. They're going to bring all the resentment at the mainstream into the community. It's going to cause all kinds of bullshit. So much gossip was being spread. You always had to be on edge. No one just seemed that loving toward one another. There were pockets and cliques. There was a lot of strife. If you don't say 'Hi,' you're a sellout. There's no straddlin' the fence. So basically, having white friends was enough to label you a sellout anyway, so you might as well not talk to anybody in the black community.*

"*I never really fit into it. I was friendly with everybody. Everybody was like, 'Hey, what's up?' But I never felt like... It was hard for me to find women in the black community, so eventually I had to go main stream socially. There were a few... The women I did mess with at school always had an affinity for the basketball players. It seemed like a lot of relationships fizzled out, not necessarily with them chasing basketball players, but the whole 'Who's Hot, Who's Not' mentality. And I still feel like black women do that even now.*

"*So I went through that, but at some point, I realized, by senior year, that I was depriving myself of what Georgetown had to offer by trying to stay in such a tight-knit group that, really, I was having a lot of problems with at the time. I just got so fed up with it, so I said, 'Why am I going to settle for this? I'm just going to open up the ducts and go where I want to go.' It started off the first week of senior year, when I decided to kick it at all these different parties. One of those parties I kicked it at was where I met Alana. Then I started dating her.*

"*I was totally cool with it. Alana and me; we were soul mates. I really loved that girl. Then toward the end of the year, the [black Greek sorority] spied us on the street one night, walking back from a bar. We had such a great night. We had been fighting for a while, not speaking. We finally decided to make up. I ended up carrying her out of the bar. It was an awesome night.*

"*We're walking down the street, holding hands. And I'm totally scared of this, 'cuz I knew how the campus police were about shit like that. Alana liked public display of affection. She didn't see anything wrong with it. She wouldn't be embarrassed to walk across campus holding my hand. That would have never entered her mind, the race issue. Me: that would terrify my ass.*

"*I remember hearing the screeching halt of brakes. And I think it was Erica screaming out the window, 'Alan, what are you doing?' It was all the women of that little group. I mean, I didn't even know what to say at that point. It caught me so off guard. And I actually did feel like I got caught doing something wrong, so I wasn't even at the point where I would defend myself. I was like a deer in headlights. Then they drove away.*

"*And here we are, it's, like, a month until the end of school, the end of four years at Georgetown, and they completely wouldn't speak to my ass. I mean, it was FUCKED UP! These people who I knew since I was a freshman wouldn't speak to me. I used to go to their rooms, order wings together during late nights and shit like that; wouldn't speak to me. I was like, 'Y'all can kiss my ass. If that's what's supposed to be loyalty, that's bullshit. I don't have to justify myself to anybody. That's a given. But if we're going to accept the fact that it's a painful image for black women to see a black man with a white woman, that still shouldn't be enough for you guys to completely end a friendship with me.' That's bullshit.*

"That carried itself out until I graduated. When I moved back to Chicago, I sort of reveled in the idea of hangin' out with a lot of my high school friends again. When you're back in your city, you sort of revert back to your high school-ish ways. Since then, I just basically have been, slowly and surely...I don't know how to say it... I guess...uh, stripping away my hang-ups, and just 'being' more instead of over-thinking it."

What Exactly Is College For?

I got into all the schools I applied to: Penn State and Northeastern, which I considered safety schools, Morehouse and Hampton, obligatory shots at black colleges, and the University of Pennsylvania and Georgetown University, what-the-hell-go-for-it pipe dreams.

I didn't think I'd get into my "dream" schools. My grades were decent, ranking somewhere right in the middle of the two-hundred-something people in my class. My two SAT attempts were not up to par. I never broke one thousand. I didn't even attend the mandatory interview with an alumnus that was required for Georgetown. The idea of going to a first-tier university was the furthest thing from my mind.

When I got the acceptance letter, I was shocked. A "name" school accepted me. The only things I knew about Georgetown were that it had a good basketball program, my favorite New York Knick went there, they had cool school colors, and Moms thought basketball coach John Thompson was a stud. And the name sounded cool. *Georgetown.* Somehow I had gotten the idea that the name was surrounded by prestige.

I applied with the intention of graduating from their business school, not because I liked business, of course. I never thought of taking high school economics. Shit sounded too damned hard. I had no idea what business courses were all about. I just knew it had somethin' to do with money. I had those notions of one day being able to take care of Moms and buyin' that forest-green Jaguar, for myself, in memory of Pops. I had a notion of having my pick of jobs with the name "Georgetown" on my resume, even though I didn't know what a resume was, or what type of job I would go for. I had a notion of meeting my future wife in college, and we'd be able to pick and choose how our kids would be schooled, not having to depend on token educational programs.

Getting that acceptance letter seemed like a godsend considering the events of the previous weeks. Moms and I were sure Pops was smilin' down on us, resting in the peace that his son had a shot at climbin' the social ladder and that someday I'd be comfortable, secure, and happy. All I had to do was say yes.

My first sight of Georgetown came in late April of my senior year in high school, upon invitation to attend their Minority Prospective Student Weekend. When I stepped out of the cab, at the main entrance at 37th and O Streets in Northwest Washington, DC, I was immediately hit with the idea of college. The buildings looked old and academic. The lawns were spacious and well groomed, the crossing bike paths traversed by cyclists with backpacks and backwards baseball caps. Students strolled along lookin' like they had some place to be, all of this behind the black granite statue of a seated John Carroll, founder of the then two-hundred-year-old institution of higher learning. The fact that it was the bicentennial year added to the buzz. It looked like what college was supposed to be. And I was supposed to be in college.

The entire weekend was well planned and much more inviting than when I went to Hampton. There was a gathering of prospective students in a large hall in one of the dorms. The upper-class presenters were funny, articulate, and people of color, mostly black. I felt welcomed. They unobtrusively went around the room to make prospective students say their names and where they came from. Nobody likes doing that, even as adults. But by the time they got to me, the ice was already broken. The atmosphere was comfortable and relaxed.

They paired us with current black students, current at the time. My lookout was CJ, a total Dwayne Wayne-type with glasses, high-top fade, and a big butt that bounced when he walked, like a character from "Fat Albert." He was cool, but he made it clear that he didn't want me clinging to him. I understood. After several meetings and workshops, it was fairly easy for visiting students to start forming cliques. Not surprisingly, I initially gravitated toward guys like me. Without actually knowing, I knew the situations of others by the way they talked, by their demeanor, and by how friendly they were, sometimes too friendly. We had the same stories. Without explaining anything, we knew. It's like we spotted each other from miles away.

I even ran into an old friend from my first year in public school in the Bronx, Alain Silverio. We would eventually become re-acquainted and better friends all throughout college. I also met a guy who asked me if I'd mind him recommending me as his roommate, another added measure of security. Little things like that added to my comfort of the situation.

The highlight of the weekend was a "Star Search" talent show, a showcase of modeling, singing, and dancing. It was incredible to be around so many young, good-looking black people and not feel self-conscious. I felt like I could be a part of something.

But it was really the parties that did it for me. Everybody was cool, havin' fun. And I'd never seen a more impressive collection of hot, black women before then. Not that I felt like I had a shot at any of them, but still. Gah-damn! And then hearing stories the next morning of the adventures of the upper-classmen. As far as I was concerned, all college students did was party and hook up. The choice was made.

Toward the end of senior year in high school, my grades fell. It was the first time in my life I got a "D" on a report card. Part of it had to do with the trauma of the week Pops died. Part of it was senioritis. Part of it was due to fact that I knew I had already gotten into college. Part of it had to do with the fact that I didn't give a fuck about Advanced Trig/Pre-Calculus.

Nonetheless, Georgetown took notice and sent me a letter voicing their concern. They recommended that I participate in a program called Community Scholars, a three-to-four week program during the summer before freshman year to help students bone up on writing and study skills. I didn't think I actually needed the program, but I went. Many of the Community Scholars had also attended Minority Student Weekend. Seeing familiar faces enhanced a feeling that I was part of the black community, something I never felt a part of in my life, or rather, felt a *need* to be a part of.

My folks never stressed any pro-black allegiances with me. We had African art in our household, and there was this sort of unspoken understanding of "blackness," but nothing that was ever elaborated. I just knew that I was black, and there were no particular attachments that went with it. After my time in Radnor, I felt like I had to *be* black, to be included in blackness. Being a Community Scholar provided that, temporarily.

The pecking order was established early on within the Community Scholars group. Freshman basketball players were the alpha males, naturally. Guys who had gone to pre-dominantly black schools, or at least mixed schools, who knew how to talk the talk and who felt comfortable enough tryin' to elevate themselves to alpha-male status, came next. They were aggressive and secure enough to attract the attention of the hottest sistas, the hottest I'd ever seen in my life, in person. Every one else was a satellite in the universe of the beautiful people, African-American style.

More than being black, for me, there was just a matter of being. A lot of folks, who comment on kids of color that go to predominantly white schools, would say that we come out confused. A long time ago, I would've taken that as an insult and told 'em to fuck off. But in a lot of ways, it's true. The confusion, for me, wasn't so much about "Who am I?" I knew damned well who I was, as much as I could at that time. It wasn't like I ever hated being black or wanted to be white. But I was deeply entrenched in what many would consider "whiteness." I liked rock music, had white friends, and had a few crushes on white girls. I was just as comfortable kickin' Public Enemy as I was Guns N' Roses. My introduction to the music of Jimi Hendrix confirmed a notion within me about the blurred lines between race and culture.

A lot of black folks didn't see it that way. Without knowing, they knew my socialization was different. *"You been hangin' around white people too long,"* never said, but nonetheless communicated. It was the little things that gave it away, like my Bronx-by-way-of-Radnor slang-speak, and my bad haircuts. I cut my own hair in high school most of the time. I didn't exactly bust crisp fades. White people didn't know that shags were way out of style. If it wasn't a Kid N' Play high-top fade, it was generic anyway. Little things like that set me a part, or at least made me feel set apart.

Everybody knew me, spoke to me, and chilled with me. We played after-hours games of "Spades" and ordered wings from the Chinese place, but they didn't actually take me seriously enough to consider me "in." It might've been because I wasn't feelin' secure and "black" enough to consider myself "in." So again, I naturally gravitated toward the black/white fence-straddlers with a shaky hold on acceptance in the black community.

Being a community scholar made freshman-year entry relatively painless. That and the fact that I'd already been away from home for the past three years. I already knew my roommate, and my academic success at Radnor prepared me to compete with the sons and daughters of corporate executives, senators, and foreign dignitaries. And I had a pass, however shaky, to membership in the black community, a card-carrying member with limited privileges.

But the Black and White theme would become one of the top three issues in my college experience, besides grades and tryin' to get some booty (In "adult" life, substitute money for grades. Do we really ever graduate?). Actually, I don't think race was so much an issue with me as it was with everybody else. I say everybody, but really, it was more of an issue with black folks, understandably.

The reasons why African-America has problems with this country are obvious enough. Personally, I've never been one to hold onto grudges; not against Bro, who broke some of my favorite toys; not Pops, who made me wear that ugly ass, green as grass, polyester suit that one Easter; not even against the mostly unintentional ignorance I encountered at Radnor. I don't know how or when I came to this conclusion, but I figured that not *all* white people are ignorant, racist, and untrustworthy of friendship. They could be more than mere acquaintances in my book. Maintaining an understanding of history, and of my "blackness," didn't have to entail cutting off personal, meaningful contact with anybody who wasn't black. I refused to swear allegiance to any set of notions about what I should do, who I should do it with, how I should think, or how I should act. I was slowly brewing into a bit of a non-conformist, at least socially. I became less and less patient whenever I got that "Nigga, what's wrong with you" vibe whenever I was doing, acting, speaking, or thinking outside of "black" protocol. Even my roommate, one off them DC brothas, started to get on my nerves as much as him having to hear Led Zeppelin's "Black Dog" blasting from my stereo got on his nerves.

"Hey hey momma, say the way you move, gon' make you sweat, gon' make you groove."

"Oh, Laaawd," he'd hiss.

Without sayin' much, he's actually sayin', "I can't believe you listen to this *white* shit." If rock music ain't your thing, I can dig that. But it doesn't make it a "white" thing. How many fucking times do people need to be reminded that any purely American music form is rooted in black music? But forget about that; it's really this simply: you either feel music or you don't. It's not necessary to take it beyond that. But of course, it's never that simple, is it? The associations we make with race aren't going away anytime soon.

Nonetheless, I didn't like feeling that vibe of being judged over bullshit. Ain't that a flip? Them white boys in high school, for their reasons, would just as soon assume that I'm not *really* black, and here I am around my own, and, for their own reasons, they're saying the same thing. I'm glad I was aware enough to start recognizing the absurdity of group thinking for what it was and is: people's overwhelming desire to validate themselves by some set of ideas that somebody else gave them.

I'd like to think that when I started to distanced myself from people who I felt were too close-minded in the black community, it was all my choice, because they somehow didn't meet my standards of consciousness and awareness. The separation was a two-way thing, though, one of those feelings you get when you think someone's goofin' behind your back. For the most part, I was cool with my fellow black students. I never had any surface problems with anybody. But do you ever get that feelin' when people smile and have pleasant small-talk with you, but you can see the thoughts in their eyes, like they're not really takin' you seriously? Maybe it was just a leftover paranoia from high school, but there were some obvious clues.

During Community Scholars, a friend of mine gave me the nickname "Tenda-Ronnie." *Then it got shrunk to "Tenderoni," then finally, "Tenda." It was right* around the time that Bobby Brown song was out. "My heart... belongs to my Roni..." She meant it as a compliment, or, at least, something that just came off the top of her head. At some point, though, it became a veiled, nudge-in-the-ribs stigma of the nice guy syndrome. I realized this when dudes would walk up to me cooing, "Hey, Tender."

"Oh, Tender, you so nice. You so sensitive. You so...Tender."

I thought they were just jealous, then girls started doin' it, gigglin' and shakin' their heads like they felt sorry for me. It was like everybody knew the punch line of some joke, and I was the only one who didn't get it. It wasn't all bad, at first. The nickname actually won me a small entourage of honeys swirlin' around me, competing for my attention. I'm not braggin'. I *wish* I could brag. I wish I could say that I straight Mack-daddy pimped d'em ho's, but that's not what nice guys do. Nice *and* naïve.

I randomly lost my virginity when I was way too young to appreciate it, but I had never actually worked to get a pay-off lay at that point. I had no idea what to do with all that ass. One of them, totally exasperated at my sloth, said, "He must be a homosexual!" Of course, she was the booga of the bunch, but that didn't matter. The nice-guy tag was firmly entrenched. The fellas out there know what that's all about. You make a great "friend," but there isn't enough asshole in you to attract thrill-seeking young ladies. An on-again, off-again relationship with a dark-skinned, feisty Dominican girl with a nasally tone like Rosie Perez kept me from feeling like a complete dead-dick in "the black community."

With social possibilities dwindling, I moved in sophomore year with a funny, cocky stud, a red-boned brotha named Art, who wasn't too shy to call himself "King Arthur," the only guy I know who thinks Toledo, Ohio is the center of the universe. Alan and his roommate moved next door to us in the same dormitory. The rest of the floor was an ensemble cast of mutual acquaintances from other freshman dorms. Our floor assumed its own identity, made up of white dudes, black dudes, Hispanic, whatever. It was all good.

I still maintained that desire to be down with the black community. I joined the Black Student Alliance, mostly as a resume builder, but partly out of obligation. I took courses in African-American literature, Harlem Renaissance, Black-Liberation Theology, Blacks in the Ancient Mediterranean: anything "black." And not out of obligation, but because I sincerely wanted to. I began to realize that I didn't need others to affirm a sense of black awareness. I was hungry to devour black history and black subjects on my own.

I felt a surge of militancy, a feelin' of neglect that I'd been goin' to school all this time and didn't know black history. I finally read Malcolm X's autobiography and books about the Black Panther movement. Intrigued by the title, I devoured H. Rap Brown's *Die Nigger Die*. I felt that surge of 'Yeah, yeah, fuck Whitey!' But I never had conflict having white friends or listening to more and more "white" music, no more conflict than DuBois predicted almost a century ago when he said all black Americans have a double identity.

But I did, and in some ways still do, suffer a sort of cultural schizophrenia. I understood that shit happened to African-Americans and is still happening to us, but it's no reason for us to be loaded down with shit, whether it's other people's racist shit or our own shit. "Black" shit is still shit. The sooner I was able to understand that, the more I was able to enjoy myself at Georgetown without the shame or guilt of feelin' like I was "selling out."

Sophomore year was my real introduction to the college experience: mainly, lots of drinking. I started goin' to white…I mean, keg parties on a regular basis, discovering that it was sometimes beneficial to be one of the only blacks in the house. Affirmative action works there, too.

'Duuuuuuude, how's it goin'? What's your name, bro'? Hey, wanna beer? EH BOB! HOUSE BEER FOR MA' MAIN MAN ROB…oh, Ron? Sorry. HOUSE BEER FOR MA' MAN RON OVER HERE!'

No, I didn't let it get to my head, but it was rather convenient at times.

When the crew wasn't gettin' drunk for free, we reveled in using our fake IDs at bars, clubs, and the liquor store. Young, drunk, and free. It felt good to be part of something other than feeling obligated, or feelin' like I was less than who I was because of what others thought. I was no longer an ABC student, or a "minority" for that matter. I just "was," more open to meeting people in classes, even if I was the only black, and extending my social network. I had friends who didn't care about anything except havin' a good time and who weren't hung up on cultural and race issues.

But then it got trickier. If my network of friends expanded, why would it have stopped with the males? I can't say I "dated" white girls at G-town, unless you call a few alcohol-induced hook-ups dating. But it was the first time I got a sense about the complexity of race and sex (I'll get much more into this later). It was like crossing the frontiers of cultural barriers: warm beer and pale, naked skin. To a lot of black folks, once you go there, your pass gets revoked. But what's even scarier to a lot of black folks is the idea that perhaps one doesn't want to come back.

Don't start trippin', now. I don't mean coming back to "blackness." What I really mean is going back to restrictions and narrow-mindedness, obeying rules you didn't make, rules that don't even make sense. I wasn't conscious enough to formulate a thesis on why it was okay to be one of the only faces of color at a keg party featuring rock music, or why it was okay to slip and slide with somebody of different pigmentation. It didn't feel bad. It didn't feel like I was doin' anything wrong. It was *fun*. Call it the allure of taboo if you will. Anyway, if that changed me in some way, I'd have to say it was for the better. The sooner I learned to enjoy myself despite everybody else's hang-ups, the better off I was.

But then there was that matter of academics. By the end of first semester of my sophomore year, it became pretty apparent that business was not my thang. Accounting I – B. Accounting II – C. Calculus – D. Business Law – D. Economics I – F, my first ever. Economics II – D. Statistics – Withdrawal. This all added up to academic probation.

Maybe I didn't apply myself, maybe I should'a worked harder. But those classes were fucking boring. I didn't understand a goddamn thing. I suppose accounting is useful if you want to be an accountant. I suppose a business major is useful if you want to go into business law, or work at the Stock Exchange, or something like that. I didn't want any of that. I just wanted to chase that image I saw on those posters that read, "Justification for Higher Education," with a garage lined with a Corvette, a Beamer, a Mercedes, and a Ferrari next to a mansion overlooking a sea shore at sunset. With a 1.4 GPA in my major, I wanted to rip that fucking poster off every wall I saw it on.

That dose of reality crashed those late 80s/early 90s, pre-recession dreams that money buys happiness and is the end-all, be-all pursuit of life. I hated getting up to go to borin' ass business lectures. I hated the work, I didn't understand it, and I didn't want to understand it. Was that what working would be like? It was the first time I got the idea that money for misery just didn't seem worth it.

After failing a class for the first time, getting on probation, and feeling like I couldn't hang, I almost gave up. I was, at least, ready to transfer, and for a brief, brief, nano-second, I thought about the unthinkable: droppin' out altogether, unthinkable only because I was practically weaned for the pursuit of education. One of the only things that kept me goin' was Moms' assurance. When I ready to give up, she said, "Baby, if for no other reason, finish school for me."

You know how moms are sometimes: comforting and undeniable. Her and Pops put so much into my education. It seemed incredibly selfish of me to quit just because of a little bump in the road.

With renewed inspiration and with a little encouragement from my mentors Bob Norris and the Reverend Ronald Wells, I did the simple thing and switched majors to classes I was actually getting A's in: English. I found myself a much happier person for the next two years, takin' classes that I wanted to take, reading books I wanted to read, and discovering that I had a knack for writing decent papers. It was the first time in my life that I was actually into my education for learning's sake, not for some outward goal, and I did much better academically.

But when the end of senior year rolled around, I watched business majors get one interview after another. Companies would come to the school and seek *them* out. Business majors who interviewed on campus always complained about receiving one rejection letter after another, but most of them ended up with a bite, comfortable in knowing that they had a job after graduation. All I did was go half-heartedly to the career center, take those "What Career Are You Best Suited For" surveys, and perform mock interviews with counselors. I had absolutely no idea what I wanted to interview for. I had no idea what I wanted to do. I took the graduate school GRE test, hung-over, but didn't take the idea of goin' to grad school seriously.

When people find out you're an English major, the first thing they say is, "You can always teach." A lot of people suggested this to me, if not just to have a job, then to be a role model that black children in the city needed to see; a young, black man with a degree from Georgetown. It was my duty to give something back. Part of me believed that. But what exactly was I supposed to give back? I was graduating from one of the best schools in the country, and I wasn't thoroughly convinced that it meant anything. The value of what I learned wasn't directly connected to the school itself, the school I chose 'cuz it sounded prestigious and had cool colors on its uniform, or to school in general.

Don't get me wrong. It was a privilege having gone to college at all. I enjoyed myself, but it wasn't exactly "Animal House" (or "School Daze," to be black politically correct). I had fun, but it wasn't a Roman orgy. I learned a lot, but I didn't know what it was all for, or what it was going toward. The prospect of graduation and the future beyond filled me with an anxiety I hadn't felt before, an anxiety that would remain for years. What the hell was I supposed to do with my life, and how would I steer people on a path similar to mine when I didn't even know where it was going?

When I was in school, I always thought about the next year. But for the first time in my life, I wasn't goin' back to school. And damn near everybody else seemed to be goin' on to work somewhere to make decent money, a confirmation of four years of hard work. The only thing I had to look forward to was the knowledge that, someday, I'd *have* to get a job. Life seemed to be a twisted game show.

"You've gone to good schools, you've had your college experience, and you have a degree. That's it. Thanks for playin'. Now get a job and have a nice life."

So much for the forest-green Jag, the downtown office, the illusion that education = social elevation. Maybe if I wanted to chase the *idea* of a "good" job bad enough, I would've. But I didn't wanna just get a job. I was too cynical and unfocused. This was when the real search began. A question mark built itself in my brain, but I didn't know what the question was, or what it would answer. I was lookin' for somethin' else.

I felt no huge swell of pride upon graduation. In Georgetown's College of Arts and Sciences, we had a mass-efficient graduation. There were too many students, name by name, to walk across the stage. "English majors, stand up. You're graduated. Now sit down. Philosophy majors..."

It was hot as hell that day, underneath the black cap and gown. I was hung-over and really didn't feel like being bothered. It was an obligation rather than a celebration. I hate ceremonies. But if it made Moms feel good, so be it. I was grouchy at the uncertainty of the future, but despite my gripes, having received an education from Georgetown wasn't exactly the worst thing in the world.

A lot of people dressed up in their Sunday best. I thought, not only was it impractical because it was so fuckin' hot, but the idea of dressing up was absurd. I threw on a ratty T-shirt, ratty, gray shorts, and ratty, four-year old Eastland loafers, the ones I used for household slippers. It wasn't some wild, rebellious gesture, but I had contempt about the whole idea that I was supposed to take all of this seriously, dressin' up like I was goin' to church, which 99% of the other black students did (and white students too, for that matter). I loved seein' the looks on the faces of my black friends' parents, that "Is this nigga crazy" look. I wore an "I dare you to say something" smirk right back. Moms didn't care. She understood where I was comin' from.

The status of being educated, the degree, and the ceremony meant more to her than to me, but she gave me enough room to be cynical. The idea that I was somehow special because I was a black man privileged with an education from a prestigious school didn't hold the weight that so many people seemed to give it. I knew there had to be something more to this game.

I met Alan at the beginning of freshman year, but we didn't start gettin' tight until second semester. We lived next door to each other sophomore year and lived together junior year with our roommates from sophomore year. We came from different sides of our little four-man clique, but Alan and I formed tighter bonds with each than we did with our roommates.

When senior year rolled around, I had to bail on them. See, you're supposed to live off-campus one year. We all lived on–campus for the first three years. My room and board were paid through the school as long as I lived on-campus. If I were to move off-campus, it would have to come out-of-pocket. Moms and I simply couldn't afford that.

I had a friend who was a resident assistant of an on-campus apartment complex. His apartment would not have been considered eligible in the pool of available apartments, so I could live with him despite the fact that I used up my three years. A fifth person was needed for that apartment, so I grabbed the spot.

Alan and the others struggled in a tiny, poorly ventilated apartment off-campus, not only with bills but also with each other. In a sense, the equilibrium was broken when I left. No matter how practical it was for me to have left, they felt abandoned. Alan relayed that to me in the middle of senior year, pointing out that I only went to their house when I needed a crisp haircut from King Arthur or when I wanted to play Alan's Super-Nintendo. It was the first time I was ever questioned on my loyalty as a friend, and it was shocking.

I was lucky to have a variety of friends and the luxury of choice in which clique I wanted to hang out with given my mood at the time. I was selfish in that aspect. If there's one thing Alan and I have in common it's an avoidance of social stasis.

At first, I thought that he was over-reacting to my aloofness. It wasn't until years later that I understood why he needed me to be more dependable as a friend. There was a lot more goin' on in his life than I ever suspected, and it had something to do with that question mark burrowing itself in my brain. Where is all of this heading?

Alan: Breakdown

"*My father moved to the city of Chicago to be an inner-city, bourgeois, black professional. That's what he got into. He had a Mercedes and wanted to live in a nice townhouse community. Our neighborhood was very diverse. It wasn't primarily any one race. It was a wide mix of people. He wanted to send his kids to private schools. Anybody who's a professional does. A part of it was also that Chicago public schools are really bad. It would be in your best interests if you could send your kids to private school. But in the process, [my father] enjoys the prestige of being able to send his kids to private school.*

"*At the same time, and it wasn't until I was an adult that I was able to understand this, he had a certain amount of resentment toward me and my sister for being, like, spoiled. When my mother passed away, he got us a housekeeper. Ever since I was a little kid, we had a housekeeper. He was resentful toward us for being these proper-talking, white-acting kids with a maid who cleans up after them and fixes their meals. He's sort of feeling like, 'Well, I never had that when I was growing up.' And in some weird, sort of sick way, he wants us to have what he didn't have, but at the same time, he's almost jealous. 'These kids will never appreciate what they have,' like we took it for granted, which we did. I mean, when we were kids, I will definitely admit that I took for granted a lot of the shit I was given. In my eyes, it wasn't nearly as much as what my rich white friends were getting. I was still at the lower end of it all, so I never felt privileged.*

"*I think a lot of the resentment comes from the fact that we were privileged, but we never saw ourselves as privileged kids. So that just has all sorts of issues because that reflects that he's working hard for his kids to feel good that they don't have it as bad as he did. Yet, we don't appreciate what he does for us. It's not that he ever said it, but we just took everything for granted and never thanked him, blah, blah, blah.*

"*It's still kind of a mystery to me. I don't know what my dad's story fully is. He hid a lot of it from us growing up.*

"*I think my dad is a manic-depressive. He just doesn't want to admit it. I think, now, he may know, but he's just in denial. And what's typical of a manic is that they go through long series of just totally being bummed out, sluggish, and lethargic. Then they'll turn around and be aggressive: strong personality. My dad totally does that. It's uncanny. He'll go through months where all he wants to do is watch Bull's games. If you interrupt him, you're pissing him off. It's fucked up. As a child, it sucked because when we needed to do shit, like have him drive us places or something, he didn't want to be bothered.*

"*There was one specific time where my sister had a project due the next day. She had to go to Walgreen's and pick up some poster boards for the project. My dad was watching television. I think I had a basketball game or something like that. He was like, 'Have Alan do it.' I can't exactly remember what led up to this, but it was in one of those slumps where he was just being a lazy fuck, and it was pissing me off. As a teenager, this is what I was thinking. So I was WAITING for him to tell me to take her to Walgreen's. I thought HE should be the one doing it.*

"So I said to my dad, 'Sorry we had to get in the way of your television time.' I said something real wise-ass. I don't remember exactly.

"My dad got up in my face and totally went off. He's never really hit me, but he was IN my face like, 'Don't you ever tell me what I should do as a father! You guys don't have any idea what I have to go through to put you guys through school, and you have the nerve to mouth off to me? You damn well better believe you're gonna take her!' He just went off. He was so offended by the fact that (A) I was so insolent (B) That I was... It was like reacting. If you try to get in the way of his form of escapism, if you try to pull him out of that little cocoon, he reacts. He panics.

"That was a really devastating thing. My dad didn't scream a lot, and he just wasn't very physical with us, so it definitely took me by surprise. He would just never do that stuff.

"I'd have plays, and he'd never go see them. Whenever we had events, he'd never go to them because he was too busy watching television. He just didn't have a legitimate excuse except to watch television, which, as a child, you can imagine, would piss you off.

"On the flip-side, he would go into these sprees where he would just be very dictatorial. He would lecture all the time, from the moment he walked through the door. He'd be spoutin' off. In fact, I'm reading this 'Great Santini' book, and a lot of it sorta reminds me about my father when he's in this state. I think that in a weird sort of way, me and my sister were emotionally abused as children, and it's something that I'm still working through, but I'm getting more of an edge on it, I guess, with reading this book and other stuff. My dad, when he goes through these phases, all his lectures would stem back to how we weren't doing enough.

"It was weird. He'd be watching ANYTHING on television. We'd be talking about Michael Jordan. He'd be like, 'Yeah, Jordan's a good player, you know, but that guy works. He works hard. And he's been working hard for a long time. That's why I keep tellin' y'all, if y'all don't start workin' hard, y'all ain't gonna have a future. Jordan has his future, but y'all ain't gonna have nothin', 'cuz y'all don't be workin' hard enough. You get okay grades, but look at you, Alan. You got a B-minus. You think you're gonna get into a good school with a B-minus? Ain't nobody gonna take you. And you're gonna be on the corner...'

"He would just totally fuck your shit up all the time. He'd take these tangents and always bring it back to how fucked up you are. It would be just like that. I'm not exaggerating.

"If you tried to say anything, you were stupid. You could never question what he was saying, no matter how ridiculous it sounded. When you questioned him, you were talking back. He was the one with the authority. He'd be like, 'See, y'all don't wanna listen. That's your problem. You talk back all the time. That's why y'all ain't gonna ever go nowhere, 'cuz you don't wanna listen to anybody. I can teach you something. I been through this. I been through private schools and graduate school. You can learn somethin' from me, but y'all so busy tryin' to think y'all know everything.' I can still listen to that voice, and it infuriates me. It just gets under my skin.

"And if it wasn't that, it would be like, we think we're white, and we're so busy trying to be like white kids, and daddy knows. 'Daddy's been around these white *folk all these years, and y'all are confused. They brainwash you up there, because y'all don't know any better. It's not your fault. Y'all just don't know any better.' It was constant belittling in very subtle ways, but it was very demoralizing. We had no recourse to do anything.*

"Granted, I can say that, and there are plenty of people out there who have gone through a lot more ordeals than we did. We had a maid, and we had it good. But I still feel like there was something wrong with the way we were raised because now, my sister and I have these tendencies to be very sheepish around people. My dad took any sort of ability for us to use our intellect. He would always make decisions for us about who we were, what we stood for, what we lacked, and if you tried to employ any sort of intellect with him, he'd cut you down. He'd make you feel stupid for trying. So that, over years and years of time, made my sister and me insecure around people. Our voice didn't mean anything.

"Of course, when you combine that with the fact that we went to private schools with WHITE kids, it certainly didn't help matters much. What I felt like my father should have been doing is trying to build us up, like saying, 'You are special. Don't ever forget that. They're gonna make you feel stupid, but you should think that you're special.' Instead, he always tore us further down. He would never try to build us up.

"I can't remember what my dad was like before my mom passed away. I do know that he used to drive her crazy the same way he drove us crazy, with the orders and the lecturing. He was SO condescending in the way he lectured us. And I can understand that now as an adult, that my mom wasn't gonna take that shit. The more you grow toward adulthood, the more you can't handle someone being condescending to you 24-7. I remember there used to be a lot of fighting about that. That's the only thing I remember.

"I DO remember that when my mom passed away, I really didn't know my dad at all. He was always out of the house, all the time, doin' doctor shit. It was devastating to think that I was going to have to spend the rest of my life with my father because I didn't know him. He was a stranger to me.

"My mom was great. I would have been such a different person had she lived longer, stronger I'm sure. My mom was so involved with my sister and me growing up. She was a chaperone at all our little functions. People loved my mother. She had a strong spirit. She was very involved in the community. I remember people visiting my mother. They absolutely adored her. She had a charisma about her. I remember that as a child.

"My dad didn't want to be bothered with socializing. Once my mom passed away, he didn't want anything to do with going to school, and going to school events, and meeting parents. He didn't want anything to do with them. It pissed me off all the time because my friends never knew my father. He hardly ever wanted to meet my friends. He never wanted to be bothered with anything. I felt really bad about that. It forced me to do a lot of growing up. I would rather seek refuge in other people's houses because I didn't know what family felt like.

"I saw all these white kids with their nice white families. They had something that I didn't, which was a family, so I wanted to sleep over at their houses all the time. I'm sure the adults knew what was up because I was over at some people's

houses ALL the time. I was like a little orphan or something. They never met my dad. He was, like, this mythic figure in my life. It was a big joke because they always heard stories [about him] through me. They didn't even believe I had a father.

"My dad, when he was in his lazy phases, would cancel surgery all the time. He might've been doing this when we were kids, and I just didn't know it. He would sleep through shit, show up an hour late, nurses calling, asking where he was, all kinds of fucked up shit. But then he would go right into his dictatorial phase where he would be up all night, getting an hour of sleep a night. He couldn't sleep. It was equally as unhealthy as sleeping too much, or watching too much television all the time. He would never sleep. He would plow right through his surgical books, piles of books, just laying around, up all night, smoking his pipe, drinking coffee, so focused, like a pit bull.

"And again, he'd be spouting off, lecturing. He couldn't help but talk all the time, a nervous spirit that couldn't be quelled. It was Dr. Jekyll and Mr. Hyde. As a child, this always happened, but it wasn't until I was older that I realized my dad had a problem; that I realized, 'Fuck!' I had grown used to that. That's all I ever knew. So I was like, 'This is fucked up!' That's when I started to think about all kinds of shit concerning my father and observe him in ways I never observed before.

"Over the years, he was really bad at managing his finances. That was always the case with him. Typically, what happens with these doctors is that they're really into doctoring, and they have wives around that sort of manage the accounts. In many cases, their wives will be their managers. My dad didn't have that when my mom passed away, so he just couldn't manage. It was a downward spiral.

"My dad was in real slump. I know that we were having money problems. Ever since I was a sophomore in college, we started having problems with money. It was really a stretch at that point. We didn't know if I'd be able to come back. I didn't know if I'd be able to graduate. It was getting really scary right around the end of my college career.

"It was right around Christmas time, right between the two semesters, senior year. I noticed my dad in a slump, but it wasn't atypical of what he was usually in. We had a housekeeper. She answered the phone and told me it was for my father. I went to knock on his door, but he wasn't answering. Then I went inside. I didn't see him, and I just got this really weird feeling because I knew he was in the house, but he wasn't answering. I was immediately overtaken by fear.

"I walked into the bathroom, and there he was, in a pool of his own blood. It was fate that I discovered him there because if it wasn't for that phone call, I would have had no reason to knock on the door, and he would've just been there for the longest time.

"It was the scariest thing ever. I totally freaked out. I started screaming and crying. I thought my dad was dead. I panicked and was running around. The housekeeper was asking me what was wrong. I couldn't even utter what was wrong. I was in a state of shock and disbelief. I finally told her dad had committed suicide, and she was trying to convince me to go upstairs. I was like, 'No, he's dead, he's

dead.' Finally, she convinced me to go up there. I walked in there and realized that he was still sorta breathing. He was in this discombobulated state. We called 911, and we took him to the hospital.

"After a while, when he recovered, my dad sort of dismissed the whole thing. For a while, he was a little apologetic about it. He was saying basically that the reason he tried to commit suicide was that his money was fucked up, that he couldn't pay our bills, and that I wasn't gonna be able to go back to school and graduate. It reached the end of the line financially, and we were just totally fucked. He kept saying for a while that he didn't feel he had a choice, and that the walls were crashing in on him, and he was sorry, but he just didn't see any other way.

"You gotta understand that my dad is a doctor. He's a surgeon, more importantly. He tried to stab himself in the chest. He bled a lot, but he didn't die. He would know how to kill himself if he wanted to, but it was definitely a cry for help.

"It was shortly after he came back from the hospital. He didn't want to see people for a while, obviously. The Chicago black bourgeois scene... I really started to have a lot of scorn for the black bourgeois and all the shit that happened because they were so merciless about trying to find out what happened with my dad. His so-called friends and associates; doctors, lawyers, professionals around the city... In the name of being concerned about my father's well being, they were just trying to get the story so they could spin it off to the community, because it's probably no more than 250 or so high profile black professionals in the city.

"I hated that. I thought that was so fucked up. It was such bullshit to me that people had to have a story, and no one could just leave him well enough alone. I remember just hating everybody for that. He suffered enough. I think it was just one of those subconscious decisions I made that I would somehow take myself out of that crowd of people. I would never involve myself with catty people like that.

"Again, it's like in school. When you have a small community like that... It's no different than any other community. It's just human nature that cattiness is gonna abound, and people are gonna try to tear one another apart. That kinda shit is gonna happen. There's gonna be a lot of competition and jealousy and envy. People are upset with their own lives, so they're gonna try to take that shit out on the community. Nonetheless, I didn't like that. That's just a little side note.

"But that was really only the beginning of it. After a while, we got it together. There was an outpouring of emotions. Family rushed in, everybody was totally one, all this love came in. It was so special. My family can be strong like that. We could hold ourselves together despite this. Money came in through the family, and we got the tuition bills paid.

"I graduated and stayed home for a while. I figured that my dad was better, that all it took was that he needed to make this big release, this rude awakening. I assumed that it would all fix its self, I guess. But it didn't. My dad caught up financially, but he still felt broke.

"He had another breakdown and just disappeared. We couldn't find him. He was missing for nine days straight. This was a huge, city-wide deal. I was on camera, on television. People were at my house everyday interviewing me and my sister and his wife. It was during Father's Day, so they were tryin' to spin it off.

"'Not everybody's having a good Father's Day. This family has been missing their father for eight days now.' It was a countdown. It was fucking ridiculous. The news of the city: nice doctor, family broken up. It was horrible, dude. FUCKING HORRIBLE!

"I just knew my dad was dead, didn't know if he was car-jacked or something, didn't know if he tried to kill himself again, and succeeded this time. I had no idea. It was so unbearable; to say nothing of the fact that it was completely out in the city. No one really knew my dad had tried to commit suicide. Everybody in the media was trying to spin it off like he got mugged or something like that, but of course we knew he was dealing with depression, so it was more likely that he tried to do something with himself.

"Finally, someone spotted him at a hotel. My father had got in his car and drove until he ran out of gas, basically. He wound up in Detroit. And thank God because, as much as I want to slam the media about this whole thing, this guy got WGN in Detroit. He was able to see the story every night on the news. He was able to see the license plate and all that stuff, so he saw the Mercedes in the driveway at the hotel. They found him in the room, and he was just...there. He lost fifteen pounds or something like that. He wasn't eating. He was just sitting there; he had a breakdown.

"Something happened and I was out of the house, but when I came home, it was all taken care of; my sister and my stepmother had already flown out to get my father. They got him immediately. I can't recall what happened after that.

"When he tried to commit suicide, they gave him a therapist. He had two or three sessions, then stopped going. He claimed he was okay and better. Again, we were like, 'Fuck, you gotta go back, you gotta do something about this.' Again, I think he tried to appease us by going back, but he really didn't stick with it. He couldn't understand why everybody would walk on eggshells around him. 'Okay, it happened. I had to get away. What the fuck is the big deal? It's over with. I'm sorry, I apologize, now let's get back to business.' He didn't say that, but I can see that the way my dad was operating, he just really didn't see anything wrong.

"That was too much for me to deal with. That was what led me to not go to law school. It was that moment, because I figured out what was going on with my dad. It wasn't the right diagnosis, really, but it seemed to me that my dad had a mid-life crisis of some sort. He just didn't want to be a doctor anymore. I think he had a genuine passion for being in medicine. I still think he does. At the time, my analysis was that he lost his passion.

"The whole thing freaked me out. I had just graduated from college; I had no idea what the fuck I wanted to do. I moved out of the house at that point and moved in with a friend who was still in school. My dad couldn't understand why I was leaving. He was pissed off because he saw this as a sign that I was leaving for good. He didn't want his son to be moving out without a job. He thought I should stay there until I had myself together, that I wasn't ready to move out. I was like, 'I gotta leave; I can't do this. This is too much for me to deal with.' So I moved out.

"I used that. It showed me that I better be in a profession... Again, I was still naïve when I came to this conclusion, but I didn't want to have a breakdown. I want to be happy. I don't want a career that I'm just doing it to do. I want to love *what I do. I didn't want to be a lawyer, so there was no way in hell that I was gonna commit to that. I had to find something else. It was around that time that I found advertising."*

Another Graduation

The best thing about graduating from college was a thousand-dollar check I received as a gift from a benefactor through my church. She helped me financially all throughout college. I never actually met the lady. She was one of those old widows who had enough money to toss my way, probably without missing it, but, I mean, I'm worth every penny. Sometimes, it's not so bad bein' a charity case.

I spent the summer not worryin' about getting a job. You could call it a clearing of the mind, if healthy doses of sweet Mary Jane could possibly contribute to clearing one's mind. Moms was cool enough not to pressure me about a job while I lived with her. I figured I pulled it out for the long haul. I deserved a break. That and the fact that it might've been the last summer in my life I would have off.

There was that possibility of teaching, something I really didn't want to do, but what the hell else does an English major do? I was in no shape to do such a thing, emotionally or professionally. I went to public school in New York City. I knew how much of a battleground it was dealing with (A) The System, (B) kids who are socially and emotionally "challenged" within that system, and (C) trying to teach the bunch who want to learn in between breakin' up fights and all the other shit teachers don't get paid nearly enough for. The problem with me was that I still felt like a kid; I still felt socially and emotionally challenged, and I wasn't thinking too highly of education at the time. How was I gonna convince kids that goin' to school was the thing to do when I wasn't even sure why? It didn't seem right for me to be role model when I still didn't know what my role was.

Eventually, my graduation money ran out, and the reality that I *had* to get a job set in. For the first time in my life, I wasn't goin' back to school. The grind of "life" began. I had no clear direction, and I was broke and jobless.

Thankfully I wasn't alone. I got close with this cat DJ Maniac, AKA Crazy Mike, my best friend Victorio's older brother. I'd known Mike for years but only as a distant acquaintance. I always thought he was too aggressive, assertive, and over-bearing, but it was exactly what I needed to help me through the post-graduation blues.

Mike's one of those guys who proves that you don't have to go to college in order to be smart. He was one of the first people I met that inspired me to focus on Life 101, the course you can't really study for, where there are no grades or finals, but tests galore. And you're never really sure whether you passed or not, but nevertheless you keep movin' on. After graduation, there were times when I felt like I had misspent the previous four years. I didn't feel any more prepared for "The Real World" after college than I did before. College seemed more like a four-year extension of avoiding reality than preparing for it. If I could've been just as smart in the game of life not having gone to college, not only could I have saved 13 Gs in loans, but maybe I could've gotten a jump on playing the game in The Real World, not the isolated bubble of the university. What the hell did I go to college for?

I often mulled over this at Mike's little bachelor pad up the street from Yankee Stadium, gazing out of his window at the densely crowded buildings of the southwest

Bronx, watching, with tireless awareness, the number 4 train pass by. My pot stupors evaporated into the best in underground dance music spun by DJ Maniac, sparking the imagination, relieving my boggled and clueless mind from the confused reality of a jobless Georgetown graduate. I had this endless yearning for something I couldn't identify.

We spent many a night sittin' on park benches around Van Cortland Park, further up where I lived with Moms, savoring one-dollar Heinekens from the bodega, waxing philosophy and talkin' shit: women, politics, the state of the world, the state of life, in ways that I'd never thought of these matters before.

It's amazing... the things you think about in the midst of aimlessness. You all of a sudden become a philosophy major. I was Plato to Mike's Socrates. The object wasn't to discover the meaning of life or to answer any profound questions. It was the questions that really mattered; the fact that we asked them; a better, free-flowing forum than any I ever had at Georgetown. Van Courtland Park was our own university, night classes only.

Imagine that? An alumnus from an educational program and Georgetown graduate, sittin' on a park bench in the Bronx, drinkin' beer from a brown, paper bag, jobless. Wasn't this what I was supposed to be getting away from?

To the casual observer, I wouldn't have appeared any different than any other brotha' from the Bronx, sittin' on a park bench, drinkin' beer from a brown, paper bag. Come to think of it, what made me that different? I had a degree. I traveled a bit, seen some of the "outside" world. But there I was, in the Bronx, sittin' on a park bench at night, drinkin' beer from a brown paper bag, tensing whenever cops rolled by, slobberin' at the Hispanic honeys strollin' down the street. What made me different from the rest of the brotha's doin' the same?

That's the problem I've carried with me ever since high school. I never really quite fit in anywhere. I did and I didn't; I do and I don't. I got by comfortably wherever I was, whether it was in the hood or on the hilltop, but I still felt outside of everything. I was back at the place where I came from. It felt good, like I slipped back into a self that hadn't existed for nine years. But I was undoubtedly a different self. Would the brotha' sittin' two benches down from me, smokin' a blunt and drinkin' a 40 ounce, be able to kick Milton's "Paradise Lost" with me? In his own way, maybe he would.

I went through a period where unless I was applyin' for a job, I purposely downplayed or neglected to tell people, especially black people, that I went to Georgetown. I didn't want anybody to think I would look down on them, like I'm some kind of uppity nigga. When I told white people, I grew tired of their responses of amazement.

'You went to Georgetown? Wow!'

I often wondered if their response was a compliment or an insult, seeing this black graduate from a prestigious school in front of them. I could look into some people's eyes and see the words "Affirmative Action" rolling across like Time's Square neon. The subtext of that, sometimes, was that they had to go to their second or third choice of schools because Georgetown gave this nigga a slot and not them. Hey, if that was the case, sorry dude, but it's about goddamn time white people started knowin' what racism is all about. And, of course, it becomes totally unacceptable when they feel they are the victims of it. Oh well, whaddaya gonna do?

Beyond those subtleties, though, I hated the idea that people responded to an image of prestige when hearing the name Georgetown, an image that I thought was overrated.

However, as I've discovered more and more, the name does open doors, no doubt. When I seriously started lookin' for jobs after graduation, I had one legitimate shot at what one would consider a job worthy of a Georgetown graduate, working at some financial place down by Wall Street. My godmother got me the interview. I didn't ask for her to hook me up, but just like everything else for me, the opportunity was there. I went to the interview more out of obligation than with desire for the job, but the job was there if I wanted it. A couple of weeks of training, and I would've been set. I could'a been on track for that image of downtown workin' I always fanaticized about.

Then I remembered Microeconomics.

I got one thing out of that interview. There's no point showin' up with your nice suit, smilin' and comin' up with your best, pre-programmed answers to questions you rehearsed a thousand times if you don't really want the job. I mean really want it. I was so listless; it was obvious that I was just goin' through motions. At one point, the lady interviewing me asked, "Do you even want this job?"

It was one of those small but key moments in life that, when you look back on it, changes the course on how and why you do things. I thank that woman for being so observant. If she had said, "The job is yours," I'd have probably taken it out of a combination of desperation and guilt, but I knew that shit wasn't for me. Even still, I felt guilty for sayin' no. I felt guilty that my godmother went through the trouble of hookin' me up. I felt guilty for turning down an opportunity to make half-decent money at a prestigious firm. I felt like I was supposed to live up to the standard of the educated black man. After all, what did I go to school for?

Feelin' more pressure to fall into a career, I sent out resumes to publishing companies. Publishing seemed the closest thing related to an English major. That went nowhere. I had taken some screenwriting and video classes at school senior year, toying with an idea to write and/or produce film and video. That never seemed like a "realistic" possibility. Most people try to back-door into the industry as production assistants. Those end up being crappy and unfulfilling jobs, so I've heard, unless you're a real predator, which I wasn't.

It took me a long time to realize that findin' a dream job out of the New York Times was a lesson in futility. I scrapped to find the ones I did. Ultimately, I ended up workin' a series of part-time jobs that didn't require degrees: filing, data entry, clerical work, messengering. The strange thing was that I actually felt "normal" working in places that didn't require a college education. Not that it was, or ever will be, my ambition to be a clerical assistant, but most of those jobs didn't require me to pretend that I liked what I was doing, and they weren't nine to five suit and tie gigs. You show up, do what you gotta do, take your ass home and get paid, not like my other business major friends who were working like dogs with seemingly no control over their lives. That ain't how 22-year-olds are supposed to live.

I even had a standard. I would never take a job where I couldn't wear my three earrings, back when it was still a big deal in a lot of companies. It was youthful idealism, but now more than ever, I know what was behind it. It was something I didn't want to admit to myself back then because it meant I'd actually have to be responsible for charting my own course. I'm not sure if there's a "normal" job on this earth that's ever gonna satisfy me.

But idealism had its price. I didn't consciously think of this, but I felt like I hadn't accomplished what I set out to do in '86, when ABC sent me away. It became an unnecessary burden. I didn't feel like I had accomplished anything that had real meaning or value. Not to mention the $13,000 in loans I was starin' at for having gone to college, another three to four thousand in credit card debt spent at college, weekly earnings of about $115, living at home with Moms in a one-bedroom apartment, and no remote possibilities of gettin' laid.

Yet again, fortune and fate bailed me out of that situation. Alain, my friend from my first year of public school and Georgetown, called me about a job possibility he knew of. The head of the Minority Affairs Department at GU knew of an opening for a graduate assistant position at a small school in Connecticut. Fairfield University was about an hour's drive up Interstate 95 from where I lived in the Bronx. If I got the job and worked for the school, they would pay for a graduate education.

Who'd turn down that opportunity? Despite my doubts about goin' back to school, the ABC mentality was still deeply engrained in me, the idea that Education = Success. The more credentials I could pour on my resume, the better. The thought crossed my mind that I didn't miss school a whole bunch, and the programs they offered weren't exactly what I was lookin' for. They had one called Educational Media, which involved education, giving more credibility to the idea of becoming a teacher someday, and some courses in video production, my favorite senior year class. That was good enough for me. I'd have a chance to get outta Moms' one-bedroom apartment, have my room and board paid in full, and I would get a weekly stipend.

I didn't take the time to think about whether this was something I really wanted to do or not. With the whole idea of education deeply engrained in me, there was, again, no choice. I didn't want to think about what Moms and others would think if I turned down that opportunity. All I could remember her saying is "Finish school for me." And there I was with an opportunity to get a graduate degree.

I applied, interviewed, and won the job. Just the fact that I had something to look forward to gave me some semblance of peace. When I received the congratulatory acceptance letter, my pithy jobs didn't matter anymore. I was happy to be goin' away to school again, even though I knew I was only delaying the certainty that I'd eventually have to come back to that buzzing yearning I had when I graduated GU, the question I couldn't find the words to formulate. But I figured, "What the fuck; maybe a couple of years of free grad school would help me figure it out."

I knew I got the position of graduate assistant of the Barone Campus Center at Fairfield University the moment I left the interview. I impressed the hell out them and myself. It was the first interview I had where I felt like I knew what I was doing and why. I answered their questions sincerely and honestly. Imagine getting a job doin' that? I also felt like the staff interviewing me wasn't lookin' at me like some kind of charity case they needed to give a break to in order to salve liberal guilt, but rather, as a competent young man who could do the job. Maybe me being black had a little somethin' to do with it, only in that they might've been hoping to bridge the gap between the University Affairs department and campus minority groups. But they never pressured me into that liaison, nor was it a condition of employment. The sly look that Jeanne, one of my future supervisors gave me after the interview let me know where I stood with her. Fitzy, the big cheese, also gave me a reassuring comment as he dropped me off at the train station to go back home, as if to say all I had to do was present myself the way they expected a Georgetown graduate would.

I guess it also didn't hurt that I went to GU with his son – lived right across a courtyard from him senior year. Funny how things work, isn't it?

I let'em know right off the bat that I wasn't gonna be color-blind, me being black and from the Bronx, and their school being in the midst of traditionally white, affluent, conservative central. I wanted to let'em know that I was aware of my difference and that they should be aware that I was aware, but that it didn't have to have an effect on how I did my job. I wasn't going to change myself in order to fit into that environment. They'd have to accept me as I was, not who they thought I should be, not who they wanted me to be. I said all of this with the utmost subtlety, of course. The fact that they hired me is a testament to how cool they were about it.

Fairfield was even more white-bred than Radnor. My experiences from high school were still fresh in mind. It was like carrying baggage from an old relationship into a new one, like setting ground rules and parameters to not get set up for falls. No matter how confident I told myself I'd be the thought of entering that lily-white, upper-crust environment again made my skin crawl a little. I was back in the game.

Georgetown was different. The university population was fairly diverse for such a conservative school, and it's on the fringe of Chocolate City. There were enough "minorities" around where I didn't feel like one. At Fairfield, there was only a tiny population of people of color: true minorities. I had contradicting feelings about being in that type of environment again. Those nicely manicured lawns, open space, statuesque trees, and an atmosphere of status, prestige, and tranquility... It attracted and repulsed me at the same time. And then I had to deal with the people, old feelings of Radnor resurfacing, having to once again get used to the curious glances and dull stares of white kids who never had contact with blacks before.

I swore I'd do things differently this time. I made rules of attitude for myself. I wouldn't be friendly with anybody who wasn't friendly with me first. I wasn't there to make friends. I was gonna do the best job I could do, get my free master's degree, and be gone. In and out. I didn't want people gettin' close to me. I didn't want people to get any kind of easy read on me. I didn't want to feel like a kid in high school again. I shut down around most people. Anything to throw them off, to save myself from some of the shit I went through as an ABC student tryin' to dodge stereotypes. Aloofness was my numbing defense against memories of high school.

A lot of people, only when they got comfortable enough with me to say so, told me I had that "angry black man" thing going. Good. That's what I wanted, a residue of the idea that I had to "keep it real." But I didn't want to be ordinary in any way, angry black man or average Joe Schmoe. I donned the funkiest sunglasses I could find and silver chains with peace signs and bullets, New York City East-Village-wear that wasn't too common on Fairfield's campus at the time. I never looked anyone in the eye (except some of the ladies, of course), never acknowledged curious glances. I got a kick out of peoples' reactions. Was I starving for attention or what?

I wasn't that pitiful, actually, but I wanted to establish my own identity, something that set me apart. *Where's this black motherfucker comin' from?* It was an idealistic, anti-thing, but also an "I'm-not-on-anyone's-side-but-my-own" thing. Being at Fairfield reminded me that there was still a lot of unresolved racial and cultural tension within myself.

During my first semester, there was a rash of incidents where anti-minority epithets were scribbled on dorm walls and elevators. There was uproar, a protest here and candlelight vigil there, the same type of shit that happened at GU and most schools across the country. You had a small number of liberal whites who sincerely denounced statements about raping and killing "minority bitches" and bringing harm to any whites in their company. Of course, campus minorities were angry and mistrustful at the administration for waiting too long to acknowledge the situation. The majority of the campus couldn't care less one way or the other. It was a microcosm of America if there ever was one.

I think the liberals were well intentioned but a tad naïve. There were buttons made about slamming racism, something about true colors, etc. It was like somethin' out of a "South Park" cartoon. There was an open mike forum to invite discussion. A few kids, black and white, invited whoever wrote those things to "discuss this in private," to a rousing applause from the audience. There was an escort service offered for women who didn't feel safe walking across campus at night. Imagine that? The easiest way to meet honeys, and I didn't participate.

This was all good. It was good that people spoke out against racist bullshit, but I thought it all boiled down to some drunken, foul-minded idiot who wrote those things as a practical joke, sittin' in his dorm room with his fellow idiots laughin' their asses off at the hoopla they created. I didn't take the threats seriously. No matter what you do, you can't do anything about people's thoughts, no matter how vulgar. It's good to be aware, but to live in fear? Fuck 'em. It's like those kids at the open-mike forum said: bring it to me in private.

I let that shit pass over me, sinking into my own zone, so I wouldn't have to form an opinion one way or the other. The incidents confirmed my neutral stance in the social game. I didn't side with well intentioned but somewhat naïve Anglos or with angry minorities, who had every right to be angry, but who sometimes over-reacted, spittin' fire at everything and everybody. I'd seen this shit before, and I knew how it would end. Eventually, the escort service died, the buttons fell off, the wax from the candles cooled and crusted, and we were back to business. The story of America.

I didn't have the awareness or the gumption at the time to explain to anyone that racial shit is always going to happen on college campuses and companies big and small, all across America, for as long as there is an America. I hadn't yet faced or wanted to deal with the permanence of racism as a part of American life.

(All right, maybe I'm being too negative. But let's put it like this: Don't look for a black president any time soon.)

I stayed to myself for the most part that first year, observing the folly of the college scene of silly drunkenness, segregated dining room tables, and mid-term stress, fondly recalling what it was like to be an undergrad that hadn't gotten a peak into The Real World yet. I wondered if they knew why they were going through all the stress and folly.

I wasn't by myself during all of this like an awkward misfit. The other grad assistants and I became somewhat of a nuclear family, out of professional and social necessity. It helps that we actually liked each other, and we related to the neutrality of our positions. Being a grad assistant puts you in a gray area between the student body and the administrators, somewhat of an authority figure to the students, but in actuality, a grunt in the big picture of university affairs. We still wanted to party and have fun just like anyone else, but the threat of getting in trouble partyin' with under-aged drinkers always loomed. Undergrads seemed to be slightly less mature anyway, so most of the time it wasn't worth the hassle.

I mostly spent a lot of time by myself that first year, periodically chillin' with the grads and a few select undergrads, briefly dating a Sicilian-hottie junior, and puffin' weed in my little studio, trippin' on "Beavis and Butthead," pondering that nagging thing in my brain, the question that wanted to come into frame but didn't.

My time at Fairfield was when I felt the most intensely conscious and disillusioned about race matters. It was easy for me to be comfortable when I had people around who either looked, or at least thought, like me. Most of the people in my life at Fairfield were white. My position at that university pretty much guaranteed that. As it was my entire life, though, I had peeps of all kinds at Fairfield: black, white, Hispanic, Asian, and gay. I do feel that need to always make that connection with people I can identify with on that minority tip.

No matter how cool I was about that, there was still this sense of guilt at the thought of appearin' to be a sellout. No one ever said that to my face. No one ever had to. At times, I felt it, like when I'd say hi to a black person and they'd ignore me or give me a disingenuous smirk, just enough to make me question where I stood with them. I didn't want to stand with anybody who would judge me without knowing me, or because I associated with this one or that one.

But in a sense, I could see where they were coming from. Dealin' with those damn little Caucasoid brats was difficult at times. One of the worst instances came during a paint-ball excursion. A couple of resident assistants wanted me to chaperone their dorm floors on a trip. RAs had to fill a quota of activities for their floors, and if it was off-campus, they needed an adult chaperone. I'd never been paint-ballin' before, but I heard it was fun, so I went. I didn't know any of the thirty or so freshmen, intimidated by me for being black, or being a grad assistant, or both. So I gave it a chance.

We were in the backwoods of Connecticut, sharing the course with all kinds of assorted rednecks. It sucked. My gun jammed constantly, I didn't score a single hit, and I got hit so hard in the chest once, I wanted to cry. It was nothing like you'd expect of an ultimate warrior scenario. To top it all off, some guy and girl got into a shouting match, apparently 'cuz he made some kind of sexist remark. She figured the best way to get back at him was to call him out as a racist, too.

"Yeah, I heard you the other night, callin' that guy a nigger... " this and that, screaming at the top of her lungs while everybody else was either in shock, acting like they didn't hear, or bathing me with piteous looks. Even the guy himself, after the tirade, came up to me and nervously tried to start a conversation having nothing to do with what just happened, as if it didn't happen, which made me question his innocence at her accusations. I haven't been paint-ballin' since.

There I was, supposedly the adult supervisor, and I felt smaller and less powerful than those freshmen. What the fuck was I supposed to say? The girl who went on the rant giggled out an acknowledgement of the weirdness while she dried her tears. It wasn't an apology. It was more like an "I know I used you to embarrass this guy" thing. I felt like the lone black guy in history class again, on the spot, the one everybody saw but didn't see. No one else said a word. The rest of that day, and the bus ride back to campus, were long and lonely.

That's basically how I felt most of the time at Fairfield, constantly straddlin' the fence between "black" and "white," feeling like I didn't belong to either because of the shit I saw on both sides. No matter how much pride I had in myself, my individuality, my thought process, my unwillingness to choose sides, my experiences at Fairfield deepened a sense of alienation that started in high school. That "normal" thing was still elusive.

It numbed me. Dealing with a lot of people, especially the kids I had to supervise, advise, plan activities with, and organize events for; I had to numb out. Some were honestly cool, but most were just snotty brats – the backwards dirty baseball cap wearin', flannel shirted, beat-up loafers with no socks wearin', rugby playin' obnoxious children of the affluent, some of whom will be future bosses, most of whom will carry on the torch of ignorance.

Numbing out was a must. Thinkin' too much about the effect my skin had on people, black and white, would've surely led to breakdown. There were a few incidents I blotted out of memory, like the time I passed three white kids at the reception desk in the campus center, questioning my own hearing and reality when I heard one of them suck his teeth and say, "Unga Bunga," or when I went to the registrar's office to request a copy of my transcript. I submitted a written request typed to business standards. The woman couldn't believe it.

"YOU typed this?"

Um, nah lady, ah got ma muh-va ta do d'at fah me. What the fuck kinda question is that?

There were a number of small, insignificant moments of ignorance that add up significantly. I'd grown used to it, but still, every now and then they hit that raw nerve first exposed as an ABC student. I'd constantly remind myself that I was getting somethin' for all of this, that one day I'd have a master's degree for practically free. That was why I put myself in the "minority" position once again. It was why

I tolerated ignorance, numbing myself to an environment that was at once nourishing and threatening to my sense of self. Never mind that I hadn't come any closer to figuring out what to do with my life after graduation, at least I'd have a master's degree. I thought that would count for something.

Until the April before graduation, I was so happy with the idea of getting a free master's degree that I never thought about what I was gonna do with it. I wasn't qualified to be a media specialist or a teacher. I took classes that were the minimum of what I had to take or what I was interested in. It turns out that I only took one video class, the main reason why I choose that field. I wasn't certified to teach, so even if I wanted to do that, I'd have to go back for more school.

Most of my classes leaned toward education, so I half-heartedly applied for a teaching position in a private school in NYC. I don't think they felt I wouldn't have been a good match when I told them, in an essay, that "Beavis and Butthead" could be used as a teaching tool in the classroom. There is such a thing as smokin' too much pot.

My feelings about the value of education hadn't changed much since graduating Georgetown. Resume building was fine, but what for? I still didn't know what I wanted to do with my life, and the questions just grew louder and bolder. I wasn't ready to commit to a career, still wondering why I bothered with school at all. I felt like I was on a train ridin' on invisible tracks. Stations kept whizzin' by, but I couldn't see the signs. I had no idea where I wanted to get off or how. I was in the sleeping car. I could hear a party in the next car, but I couldn't open the door. It was locked, and I felt stuck. I was bored and had no enthusiasm about life beyond the drudgery of making it through days. Whatever enjoyment I experienced was drowned out by the angst of aimlessness.

I kept lookin' at the future without actually seeing it or even thinkin' about it. All I had was two degrees and a persistent, nagging feeling. Despite my misgivings, my experiences opened doors, but the downside was that I had to numb myself out a lot, internalizing frustration without a clear focus on why I was doing it all. I began to question the worth of that which started this all for me: ABC. I questioned the worth of having degrees. I questioned everything my life was about for the previous ten years. I questioned my very existence.

Suppose I stuck with the idea of advancement, the pursuit of a high-paying job in a top company. I'd always be the minority, always feelin' like that skinny, black kid in high school; the "smart" one, the one people saw but didn't see, the one people accepted but didn't connect with, the one who may or may not be a quota-filler, who may or may not have a glass ceiling over his head no matter where he went, the one always reacting to the reactions of my skin.

Where does the doubt end; the doubt in self, how self relates to others, how self gets ahead, what self is advancing toward, and why?

Another graduation. Another hot day. Another day of me not wanting to be bothered with it all. My peeps felt a lot more pride than I did. One of my boys asked me, "Damn, you're graduating, and you got a master's degree. Why you so grouchy?"

Well, yeah, I was on another dry spell, but it was more than that.

Moms was beginning to understand where I was comin' from. The night before, at a dinner dance for the graduates, she got a little taste of the type of shit I went through. At some point during the evening, some typical, arrogant, snotty, rich, seventh-ring-off-hell Connecticut Anglo bitch dissed Moms over a seat at our table. I don't think I need to tell you how fast any self-respecting, quick-to-jump-on-yo-ass black woman will respond to such rudeness.

I immediately pulled her to the dance floor. I didn't want that scene to get ugly. Moms said, "I'm really starting to appreciate what you had to deal with all these years."

Yeah, no shit. You'd think a fella would be happy having a master's degree. But I was looking beyond that, and saw nothing. Still no idea where I was going with all this, what I wanted to do, what made me feel, how I would overcome debt, or what really made life worth livn' at all.

Corporate America, Man

"There was a lot of shit that happened at Leo Burnett (an advertising agency) that was very, very, fucked up. It was a very difficult time for me. I've had quite a bit of difficult times in the last five years, going from living with my dad and his wife, to working at Leo Burnett, to being in Atlanta for two years, starving. But Leo Burnett; I'll never forget the kind of shit that went down at that place, which really bothered me about corporate America.

"I always felt, overall, that going into the creative side of [advertising]; you wouldn't have to deal with the sort of politics that I dealt with in my department at Leo Burnett, which is very true in large part. Being in the creative department, the creatives are shielded, in many ways, from a lot of the bullshit that other people have to put up with. They're shielding the people who come up with the ideas, like, 'Don't bother them. Let them do their thing. Don't stress them out too much, 'cuz then they won't be creative, and then they're no good to us.' So that's why, when leaving Leo Burnett, I always knew that there was a better road out there.

"But even still, within that, I had this boss, Kurt, the assistant to the vice president, who was a gay, Jewish dude, and his boss, Will, the vice president, was also gay, and they sort of stood together. I thought that Will, in many ways, was emotionally unstable for the job he was taking care of, and Kurt was, like, the bully, like the chief of staff, almost. He was Will's right hand man. They had a huge responsibility. Our office just never got any respect. We were the Public Relations department, and the company just always thought that PR was extra. They didn't really see any merit to our office, so they were really hesitant to allot money to us, and even more hesitant to promote appropriately. But I felt like my two bosses were doing the work of two vice presidents. It was fucked up.

"I don't know what happened to put us in such bad standing. I sort of buried a lot of what went on in that situation. After I was there for about six months, it really became evident that my boss didn't like me. At the time, I was naïve. I was only a year and a half outta college, so I was in this 'Why don't you like me' mode, which is the worst mode you could be in, in corporate America, as a black person. The more you continue to ask that question, the more you will be disappointed when people don't like you. It WILL happen. Even still, it's something that I haven't completely embraced yet because, as a black people, the only way to make it is to be very aggressive and not give a fuck about what people think of you. In the end, they're gonna have to realize that what you're bringing to the table is good work, and they can't afford to get rid of you. As much as it pains them, they know that they have to recognize you as an asset. Otherwise, if you're in this timid, trying-to-abide-by-them-all-the-time [mode], they can push you aside. They can beat you up as they choose. They'll eat you up and spit you out.

"So my boss... I think he really didn't like me in large part because I was so obliging to him, and he really had no way of chastising me without looking like an asshole. He felt that I was being manipulative in that regard. He was a psycho, a paranoid motherfucka. This guy was gay, and the way he dealt with it was by being a stern, sorta hard-nosed dude, but in his spare time, he was this 'Aaah, you go *girl' effeminate guy. But in the office, he couldn't play that. Both of them had a lot of emotional problems going on.*

"One of the first instances that occurred was that I told somebody in the office that Kurt and Will sorta freaked me out a bit. I didn't know what corporate America was like at the time, but the next day, THE NEXT FUCKING DAY, I was called into Will's office, Kurt's boss, and he closed the door. This motherfucka never talked to me because Kurt was our buffer. He was like, 'Alan, I've been hearing disturbing reports about how you're afraid of me? You feel uncomfortable about me? I just want to let you know that I don't want this to be an office where people are afraid of one another. I want this to be an open office, where people are free to speak, and we have an open door policy, and you can come in here and talk any time you need to. But more so than you just being afraid of me, because we don't have a lot of interaction, I hear you're afraid of Kurt, and that's even worse because he's your immediate boss.'

"I was so freaked out by this that I didn't know how to respond. I didn't know how he found out about it, first of all. Secondly, I don't want to have my shit out there like that. I don't remember exactly how I answered his questions, but I was like, 'Well, no, I'm not afraid of you, not at all. Granted, for the first four months here it's been tough for me to adjust to stuff, but that's natural for any job, so it'll take time for me to get comfortable around everybody, but to answer your question, no, I'm not afraid of anyone.' He ended it up by saying that if I ever wanted to talk to come to him.

"Then I realized what had happened. Again, it was sitting there right in front of me, but I refused to accept it. It was this girl that I knew, a white girl. She was about a year and a half older than I was. This girl was so fucking cool. I still think she's cool, even though she played me. SHE told him. I told her this at 6:30 at night after everybody was pretty much leaving, and he called me into his office at ten in the morning the next day. I could never put it together. I thought there was no way that she could have conceivably gotten the information back to him that quickly. I just never thought of her being the culprit. But it was her job to befriend the interns in the agency and report back because she was close to us in age. She could disarm us if she needed to. She was the eyes and ears. If she heard any rumblings going on, it was her job to report back to the establishment.

"I was like, 'Fuck!' It's foul as hell that that shit happened. It taught me, and other events taught me, to keep my fucking mouth shut. Don't tell anybody in the office shit 'cuz they ain't my friend. I still hadn't learned my lesson yet because I've always been someone... My problem is in life, and I don't necessarily see it as a problem... I don't see it as a problem per se, but I'm always open with people. If I meet you, you're my friend. I could talk to you and be personable with you. I don't distinguish between worker and friend. That was the thing I had to learn.

"I learned to always sort of never show your emotions in the office. That's why you sorta have to be peppy all the time. You don't want to look pissed off or bummed out about shit because that draws attention to you. Then people want to know why you look so upset. Then it creates more problems, so you'd be better off showing smiles than letting people know how you feel, because that got me into trouble at Leo Burnett all the time. People used to talk about how I looked upset,

and 'Why are you so upset? Why aren't you happy?'

"One of the things that was really rewarding to me about leaving Leo Burnett, and I realize this more and more in hindsight, why my boss disliked me so much, was because I was really good at getting along with everybody in the office. Everybody just sorta liked me. I went from being this really shy, coy guy who didn't talk to anybody, who always had a scared look on his face, to being Mr. Popularity. I had people laughing throughout the office at all times.

"That's why my boss didn't like me. He knew that if I continued yappin' and runnin' my mouth every time he wanted to yell at me for not doing my job right, and I went off and told two or three people it would make him look bad. He'd say, 'Shit's gotta be done in the office, so you're fucking with me by running your mouth to all these people.' There were instances where this issue came up. He just couldn't stand that. I was very miserable at Leo Burnett until the last two or three months, before I finally began to get the rapport of my co-workers.

"Another thing that happened was with this girl Devree, who was the only black girl in the office. I remember her and Kurt used to...man... Oh my God, they fucking clashed, but she had the attitude I'm talking about. She didn't give a fuck. She was like, 'I do good work, and I'm gonna speak my mind. And if you have a problem with that, fire my ass. But I'm not gonna lay down for you if I'm doing my job.' I used to admire her a great deal. She was, at the time, 24, 25 maybe, but she was kickin' much ass in that fuckin' office. They just had these shouting matches. God, Kurt just didn't know how to deal with this powerful, strong black woman, and he was gay, so his manhood was threatened all the time with Devree.

"One time, I was in his office, and we were shootin' the shit. I did fear him in many ways because he had a lot of fucked up shit going on. But we were talking, and I don't know how the subject of race came up, but it did. So he was like, 'How was that for you in college? Being at Georgetown and everything?'

"I explained to him how it was difficult coming from a big private school and going to Georgetown, where a lot of black people had not gone through the same sort of thing I went through. I was brought up with no exposure to black people, and black people at Georgetown had a lot of exposure to other black people. That was offsetting. I had to play this game where, well, was I in the black community, was I in the white community? It caused a lot of strife, blah blah blah.

"He was like, 'Wow, that's interesting because I joined a fraternity while I was in college, and I had a problem with that too, because you had to be a man...' He didn't say he was gay. He never would speak on it, but everybody knew it. He was like, 'They expect you to fit into this whole male, testosterone, jock mentality, and that wasn't really me, but I had to sort of play that game, so I can understand. I can relate to you on that.'

"I was very happy about that. I was bonding with my boss, and it was cool. After being there for seven months, finally having a real conversation. It was good.

"This motherfucka went back to Devree, and told her. THAT DAY he told her everything we talked about.

'Alan said the most interesting thing to me,' he told her. 'He said that he has, *like, problems, with the black community not accepting him, and in many ways, he feels more comfortable around white people than he does black people. What do you think about that, Devree? I mean, as a black woman, how does that make you feel?'*

"THIS MOTHERFUCKA was tryin' to divide us! He wanted Devree to be like, 'Damn, SELLOUT MOTHERFUCKA! What the fuck is he talkin' about being around white people?' He wanted to DIVIDE our asses. He felt threatened by Devree to begin with, and he knew we were tight. I didn't like her at first, but around my seventh month there, I started hangin' with her. He didn't like the fact that his young intern was hangin' with Devree, 'cuz now she was wielding power by having me help her out on a lot of projects, and I'm his intern, not her's.

"This subject came up many times in the office. 'These are not your interns, Devree, their mine, so don't try to get them to do your work assignments.' So when telling her time after time didn't work, he decided to pull the oldest trick in the book: divide and conquer. He gets this precious information out of me about race relations, then he goes back and feeds her, thinking that she's stupid; this 'militant' black woman, like, 'Fuck Alan, he's a sellout. I don't want to hang out with him anymore.' So that'll serve his purposes, and he wouldn't have to worry about her usurping his power.

"Devree told me about that, and I just couldn't fucking believe that shit. To say nothing of the fact that that was some very personal shit I told him. I didn't want her to hear that because now it does sorta make me look fucked up to her, you know what I'm sayin'?

"I thought, 'not only did it not work, WHITE MAN, but you made me closer to her.' When she told me that shit, we were closer than ever. That was my girl. It's a shame that we had a falling out because I have nothing but utmost respect for that girl.

"She just played my ass in the end. It just breaks my heart [Alan shakes as if he were suddenly chilled]. I'll never forget the day she told me that information about Kurt because, again, I was in this whole why-don't-you-love-me state of mind. When she told me that, she was enlightening me to the fact that these motherfuckas just don't give a fuck about your ass, and they'll tell your most dearest secrets and sell them on the market if they have to, to suit their own purposes. That's how devilish their asses are. At least in our office. Will was a tyrant in himself. He beat Kurt, Kurt would beat Devree, and Devree would beat me. Shit just flows downhill.

The problem I had with her initially was that she had this fucking German boyfriend that she would talk about incessantly around the office. She was always talkin' about drinking wine and shit, and I thought, 'Black woman tryin' to show off how cultured she is with her white man.' I thought that was bullshit. I didn't like that. It took me a while to realize what she was all about. I didn't think she had any soul. Ironically enough, she was thinking the same thing about me.

"So she told me about that Kurt shit, and we were rappin' and rappin', and we had a long-ass talk about it. We were friends after that. We started hanging out. We agreed that we would be a team, give each other information. You gotta have a friend like that in corporate America. It just so happens both of us were black.

"*Something happened one night after work. Her boyfriend was out of town, so she invited me to go out. Again, I was pretty naïve back in the day about a lot of things, including women. What I didn't realize was that she was inviting me over because she wanted to get her freak on. So we were talking. She had her wine set up. Jazz was playing. She was trying to SEDUCE me on the sneak tip. We were supposed to hang out at her place then go to this party, which we never made it to. We're drinking on her love couch, she's all sprawled out, ain't but so much room. So I kept saying, 'Devree, are we gonna check out this party?' She's like, 'In a minute, in a minute. Don't rush. The party's gonna be there.' Aawwww shit, I thought.*

"*We got to talkin' about how she felt being in corporate America, and race shit, of course; how she had to cut her hair and wear glasses because too many brothas were sweatin' her. I was like, 'Am I supposed to be impressed?' Our date started off with her showing me pictures of what she used to look like, including some nudes.*

"*She was telling me about how some guy in the mailroom used to always harass her. It got to a point where she talked to the authorities and threatened to have him fired. I don't know what the story was, but I think part of it was that she, and black women in general, don't want to be viewed as trash, like you can talk and act any way you want to with them because black men would never talk or act like that with white women. I think black women don't want to feel like their worth is less than that of white women. On top of that, she was telling me about how her father has a whole library of how-white-men-oppressed-us books, so that also adds to her thinking, which is funny because she was dating a German guy.*

"*We finished off this bottle of wine, went out, played pool. She was insulting me because she thought of me as this bourgeois motherfucka, and I thought of her as bourgeois, so we were always dissin' each other about how bourgeois we are. I wanted to play pool at a nice club, pool joint. She's like, 'That's for yuppies. Your bourgeois ass wants to go to a yuppie joint. I'll take you to this hole-in-the-wall in Bucktown, and we'll play some real pool.' I had never heard of Bucktown before her. She was this Bohemian black chick who was into all this culture shit. I was like, 'Ya know, you're always just tryin' to fake that shit. You're a phony motherfucka.' She was always dissin' other people for being too straight-laced. I couldn't stand it.*

"*She was very judgmental to start off with. She was like, 'I'm into all my little cultural things, and the problem with the rest of the world is they're too mainstream, and I'm into my exploration of different music and shit.' It was just so phony to me. If you're into that shit, that's cool. But you don't have to be judgmental about other motherfuckas or else you're just as guilty as those so-called yuppies or mainstream motherfuckas that you're dissing. Do your thing and shut the fuck up.*

"*We finally agreed to go to her little hole in the wall place and play some pool. She said she could beat me. I don't remember who won the game, but I was talkin' shit, and she was SHUSHING ME! We're in this hole-in-the-wall joint, and she's shushing me because I'm talking too much shit. I was like, 'Now I know you trippin'. All this shit you were talkin' in the car about me being bourgeois, and you can't even talk some mess up in here playin' pool?!?'*

"*She's like, 'I know the woman here. She's a sweet, Ukrainian woman, and she owns this place, and you know...' She acts like she's this alternative, grungy, Bohemian chick, but she can't even hang out. She apologized to the Ukrainian owner. I was like, 'What the fuck are you doing apologizing for me? I don't need you to apologize. What, are you ashamed to be out with me or some shit like that?' She's like, 'No, now you gotta understand.' And she starts explaining this whole story about this Ukrainian woman, and how she owned this bar for ten years, and she remembers when she broke her arm and still came in. I was like, 'I don't give a fuck about that shit. I'm sure she's a sweet woman. Nonetheless, you don't gotta be apologizing for me!'*

"*So we got back in the car, and we're sorta arguing about this. That's when I started lettin' it all out. I was like, 'You know, Devree, you trip me out. You try to perpetrate like you're this, this, this, and this. But really, when it comes down to it, you're a lot of talk.' She started gettin' really defensive. I don't remember the exact words that were exchanged, but I started breakin' it down because we were both fucked up. I was like, 'You wonder why motherfuckas don't like you at the job, because you play these games.'*

"*This was right after I read The Celestine Prophecy, so I knew all about how we pull people into different dramas: poor me, aloof, interrogator, and intimidator. She's an interrogator, on the verge of being an intimidator. So I was like, 'That's how you try to get attention from people, tryin' to act like you know everything and be very judgmental, and that's a problem you gotta address.' She was freaked out. She immediately went into poor-me mode. The book talks about that. Once you bring somebody to awareness, it's a rude awakening. You can't deal with that shit, when you see the truth in your face like that. I went off on her.*

"*She was like, 'What kind of person do you think I am? I can't believe you've been harboring all these thoughts about me all this time. Jesus Christ!' It went on and on. Finally, I must have laid out two or three different things she does in her life that's fucked up and that she needed to take care of, from being judgmental to being very commanding in the office. 'Do this!' Never asks please. Never says thank you. She's like, 'What are you talking about? I'm so nice to you guys.'*

"*I'm like, 'No you ain't. You should hear how them motherfuckas dog you out. You're always commanding people. You never treat people as human beings, and its all part of this problem you have. You got this false sense of self-importance that you need to take care of.' I just kept breakin' the shit down. She was in fucking tears. I couldn't believe this woman was crying. When you see her around the office, you'd think she was bad as hell. No one could tell fucking Devree what to do.*

"*Her last straw was, 'Well, fine then. I guess you're going home celibate after all, aren't you?' I was like, 'Ah, see, that's cheap. You had to go there. Yet again proving what I'm talking about. When you can't win, or get attention by the other means you're used to using, you gotta pull the sex card in hopes that that's gonna get me to succumb to your way.' She lost it.*

'*GET OUTTA MY CAR. JUST GET OUT!*'

"*I was like, fine. I just got out, closed the door behind me. I was only five blocks away from my house anyway. I was like, 'Fuck it, I'm going home.'*

"She drives up next to me. 'Get in the car. I can't have you walking home, but you gotta apologize for that shit 'cuz that wasn't right.' I was like, 'I'm sorry that you had to hear it that way, I really am. I didn't intend for it to go this far, but I felt that I really needed to tell you these things. I'm just lookin' out for you. I want you to be the best that you can possibly be. You gotta understand. I'm not trying to be malicious here. I don't get off makin' people cry.'

"So the next day, I called her up. I felt bad about it. I was like, 'What the fuck did I do? I mean, all the shit I said to her; she WAS my superior. She could have made life pretty fucking difficult for my ass in that office. What am I fuckin' gonna do,' I thought? So I got outta bed and called her up. I said, 'Devree, I know some shit went down last night.' She was like, 'You know what? I was so fucked up I don't even remember what happened. Oh, God, don't even worry about that shit.' I was like, okay, whatever. I thought, you know the deal, but your ass still ain't gonna try to recognize, and that's on you, 'cuz I told you the shit, you can listen to it or not. Yeah, it didn't happen. That's right. You can bury that shit deep into the recesses of your memory. But I know what's up.

"The thing that fucked it all up, and this is some unforgivable shit... Two weeks later, this other homosexual, a black dude that was in the office... He was the real sassy type. We went out for a couple of drinks. She said something to him in the office, and he snapped back at her, whatever; some typical, catty shit. She didn't approve of it. We would always just accept it. 'That's just Devree. She's pissing me off, but that's her.' So, she said to this guy, 'No, you're going to apologize to me.' He wouldn't apologize.

"So we went out later for drinks. It was five of us, including interns. The conversation came up again. She was like, 'I'm just letting you know, Eric, that I wasn't trying to be rude in the office, but you really should work with me on this because I'm the intermediary between you and Kurt. I will certainly do everything within my power to help you, but if we're not working together, I sure as hell can do anything to hurt your ass. All it takes is for me to go to Kurt. So I'm just letting you know.' She says that kind of thing, but then she comes back down like, 'I'm not trying to start any trouble. I just want us to work together.'

"He says, 'Devree, who do you think I am? I'm not gonna just bow down to you. That's not how people act. That's not right. That's bullshit.' She's like, 'Eric, like I said, I don't want to cause any trouble here, but if you wanna piss me off, I can...' It escalated and escalated because he wasn't gonna lay down for her. Finally, she was like, 'Alan. Ask Alan what kind of person I can be like.' I was like, 'Devree, I'm not getting in the middle of this.'

"She pulled me aside and was like, 'Alan, you gotta back me up on this. All the times I've stuck up for your ass in front of Kurt, and there have been a lot of times you don't know about... You better go out there and tell this motherfucka that he gotta apologize to me and show me some respect.' I'm like, 'Devree, how can you ask me to do some fucked up shit like this? This is between y'all. It's bullshit, anyway. You need to just chill out. Let's have a drink and squash this shit.'

'No, no, no, no. You better show your loyalty to me right now.'

"Corporate America, man. They expect shit like this. Devree was acting no different than what she'd been taught by her superiors and what they'd been taught.

It all floats down the chain. This was pretty much her first job out of college, so she didn't know any better than what she learned over the last year and a half. She's expecting me to go out there as an act of loyalty and tell Eric, '[Ghetto voice] Yo, man. You know... She be trippin' and shit sometimes, but just to make things ahight, why don't you go over there and apologize to her.' That's what she wanted me to do. Come on, I thought; she's crazy!

"She stormed outta the bar and made a complete ass of herself. She was too drunk anyway, so she did a false exit and came backing again.

"*'[Exasperated] Okay...phew! I'm cool now. I had to take a walk, but I want you to apologize to me.'*

"Again! She wouldn't drop the shit. Everybody's like, 'Damn!' I pulled her to the side. '*Devree, you're really making a fool of yourself. I'm just telling you as a friend. You just need to end this shit and let it go.*' She wound up leaving for good. Everybody laughed at her ass.

"A week later, I'm getting ready to leave. My internship was ending. I went out with her again for drinks. Then afterwards we decided to pick up her boyfriend from his job. So we go down there, she's calling [him] from the phone in the lobby. She's like, '*Okay...no honey, it's gonna be okay. Don't worry about it.*' I'm like, '*What was that all about?*'

"*'Well, he kinda doesn't like you anymore. I sorta told him you were spineless and don't have any backbone. He thinks you're a wimp now and doesn't want to be around you.*'

"*'WHAT THE FUCK ARE YOU TALKING ABOUT? WHAT KIND OF SHIT IS THIS ABOUT,*' I asked her.

"It dawned on me all in one fucking moment what had happened. Because I wouldn't stand by her in that little confrontation, she took that as me being weak. But really it was some BULLSHIT! I was tryin' to help her out by not making it into a fuckin' spectacle, which she was making it into.

"I didn't know where to start because she told that to her man, and he was on his way down. I had many words that I had to exchange with her, but I couldn't do it in that short amount of time. I was like, '*Fuck this shit. I'm outta here.*' I just walked away. I didn't know how to deal with the situation.

"Here I am, told this bitch off three weeks ago, made her ass cry, reduced her to nothing, and she's calling me spineless, like some pussy motherfucka because I didn't have her back at a time when she was making a complete fool of herself? We had nothing to say to each other again. She went out of town for a few days. I never talked to her again. I never got a chance to clear that shit up. There was no argument, no chance to let it out.

"I'm over it by now, of course, two and half years later. Nonetheless, I still have some respect for her despite her stupid personality traits: her false sense of importance, loyalty bullshit, and race shit. Typical shit. Catty, nonsense, lame shit that had us fighting against each other when we should have been working with each other.

"There's no need to get mad or place blame when it comes to the situation with black men and black women. It's too complicated. Who am I to judge? I say, '*If I'm going to be willing to overcome your shortcomings through no fault of your own, you overcome mine.' Black men and women need to be supported.*

"I can't get mad for all the years of conditioning we've had to put up with. It hurts me. But I'm always asking myself, 'What's my role in this?' The black community has a lot of self-hate going. But do I throw my hands up fatalistically? On the other hand, is it my job to carry the burden of centuries of self-hatred and maybe end up not dating at all? It's something I'll never figure out."

Complicated

I'm gonna detour a little bit after Alan's segue from the shit of corporate America to that peculiar "relationship" he had with one of his co-workers, a black woman. This next topic is complex and dubious to discuss, but I'd like to take a crack at putting the magnifying glass on places that not many want to venture. For guys like Alan and I, and his co-worker Devree, and thousands, maybe millions more men and women out there who break granitized social taboos, it's unavoidable how concepts of race play into personal relationships, whether it be white on white, black on black, male/female, or all other combinations in between. It's something that I may never come to any peaceable settlement on, peaceable in the sense that others would see things the way I see them, but I know one thing for sure: this country is still very fucked up when it comes to how blacks and whites perceive each other, and the sexual component of racism, with its resulting affects, are inextricably locked into the American psyche.

All I can do is look at my own experiences and observations to try to shed some light on what I believe to be this unavoidable truth. I really started to try to find some honesty within myself based on two separate, seemingly contradictory conversations I had with two of my closest friends back around the time I was in grad school.

The first was with Val, my co-grad assistant at Fairfield, an Italian from New Jersey. When we first met, Val and I established an immediate bond, at first primarily for the sake of a good working relationship, but ultimately as close friends. We weren't afraid to let our minds connect sincerely and openly. She was the one person who knew most of my calamities with women when I was in grad school. One day she questioned me on something that hit a nerve I didn't know was exposed. She asked, "Ron, how come I never see you go after black women?"

Fast forward about a year and a half later. My man Victorio, his girlfriend, and I are at the Hammerstein Ballroom in New York City, checkin' out these DJs called "The Chemical Brothers" in concert. Their type of music, an acidic, electro-psychedelic dance blend, tends to draw eclectic crowds, the 90's version of techno-hippies, but most of them are nonetheless white. Victorio's black, Puerto-Rican and Indian, and Sharice, now his wife, is high-yellow black. Throughout the evening, they noticed a few white girls checkin' me out, tryin' to make themselves noticeable on my radar, but I just wasn't feelin' all that outgoing that night, so I mostly ignored them (for there are never shortages of opportunity). After the concert, Victorio said, "Ya know, I'm glad you're not the type of brotha that dates white women to the exclusion of all others. Otherwise, that place would've been a virtual gold mine for you."

Somewhere between Val's question and Victorio's statement lies a truth that's hard to get at. The simple answer to Val's question was that there weren't that many black women at lily-white Fairfield to begin with. Just because there were a few, was I only *supposed* to be attracted to them? Well, there were a couple of sistas I was diggin', who, of course, already had boyfriends, and you know that becomes the hands-off cue for nice guys like me. And there's something else I've observed in my time: when I'm really feelin' a sista, in the physical attractive sense *and* the potential for similar vibes, more often than not, they're only into white guys. Go figure.

I don't remember how I answered her question, but looking back, it was just a male, his urges, and the numbers: who's feelin' me, am I feelin' them, and are they available? I guess the ofays were favored in that equation.

As for Victorio's statement, he was pretty much right also. My first kiss was with an Asian girl. The second girl I ever kissed was white. The first time I got laid was with a black girl. I've had a thing for all types of women. I never really thought much of it growing up in the multi-ethnic Bronx. At the same time, when my friends and I were at that concert, I always had this one thought in the back of my mind: if I did kick it with one of these white girls, what will my boy and his girl think? My question was answered after the show when he stated that he was glad I didn't chase white girls, like he was relieved that I lived up to some kind of acceptable standard that black men are supposed to live up to. Was that what kept me from being outgoing that night, or was I just not feelin' it anyway? Don't matter now, but the point is, as much as I've always thought that it's no big deal when you like somebody whose skin is different than yours, it does matter, if not to you or me, to those who see things differently, and the effect, however subtle, still affects.

Somewhere along the way, these things get complicated. For me, it started in high school when Moms came to visit me junior year. She noticed my roommate and I, a Hispanic dude, had a poster of model Carol Alt on our wall. In complete disbelief she asked, "Ronnie, why do you have to have a poster of a white woman on your wall?"

I really didn't think twice about it back then, but in retrospect, I think to myself, "Yeah, why *did* I have that on my wall?" It wasn't like I was jerkin' off to it every night. As a matter of fact, I *never* spanked the wank thinkin' about Carol Alt. I really didn't even think she was all that. It was more about the idea that as a teenager with raging hormones, I was *supposed* to have a half-naked lady on my wall. But honestly, I didn't even think to look for a poster of a black woman.

Once I got to college, it started to dawn on me that there was more to this race and sex thing than I ever gave thought to. Moms loved that feisty, dark-skinned Dominican honey from G-town, the one who never really wanted to officially call me her boyfriend, but she also knew I had no problem with white girls. Moms and I have had many a discussion on it, her half-joking, 'So, how's ya little *white* girls doing?' All the while, I tried to stress that it didn't matter if the girl was white as long as she was cool. But it did matter. And it does matter.

The complications continued after years of experience and observation, seeing how some black women react to the sight of a black man with a white woman, anger and resentment radiating from their intense glares. White guys react pretty much the same way, but without the same bite, as if they don't like it but accept it. The site of a white guy with a black woman arouses just as much curiosity but much less tension. Even me, as cool as I think I am about it all, I sometimes catch myself doin' a double-take at the sight of an interracial couple. Curiosity always seems to be in the equation.

It wasn't until grad school that I began to realize the gravity of it all, the raw emotions this thing arouses in people, particularly white dudes and black women. My relationships with two women, one white and the other black, illustrate these complexities. I use the word relationship loosely, as sex was not involved in either, but this fact illustrates my points even further.

The first involved Amber, the one woman I grew closest to at Fairfield. When we first met, I had a concrete wall 20ft. high and 3ft. thick wrapped around my life. It was the beginning of my second and last year. I just wanted to get school over with. Plus, a relationship I was trying to build with a senior fell apart in a nasty way, so I really wasn't tryin' to make any new friends, female or otherwise, but Amber was pretty persistent.

A visit to return a hammer she had borrowed from me turned into a "Hey, how ya doing" return visit. And another. And another. At first I thought she was just another white girl curious about brothas, so I didn't take her very seriously. I thought she was good-looking, but I wasn't necessarily knocked out by her, so there was no real urgency about gettin' close to her. But since she was so persistent, mission number one was to find out if she was available. She had two boyfriends at the time, so I thought (A) She either wanted some chocolate to complete the hat trick, or (B) She just liked hanging out with me. Well, when we were dancing in my apartment one night, I made a move on her and she skillfully avoided it, so I figured I wouldn't waste any time chasing a broad who had two boyfriends and who wasn't down for whatever in moment that was made for that kind of thing. That would make her the pimp and me the ho. So I just rolled with the friend thing. I was playin' the hermit anyway, and if she happened to swing by, whatever. All in all, I did enjoy her company.

At some point, it clicked that this was one cool chick, like hangin' out with one of your homies, a totally fuckable homie. It was the first time that I grew to be friends with an attractive woman that I wasn't necessarily concerned with fucking. I always kept that possibility open, of course, but it wasn't an objective. We bonded intensely above that level. I even remember the moment when it was sealed, at least in my mind. It was during one of those occidental visits when she was still on the periphery of my consciousness.

I threw on the Red Hot Chili Pepper's *One Hot Minute* album after she came over one night. I hadn't really paid that much attention to her, as I was doing whatever it was I was doing, but in the middle of "Aeroplane," I looked over at her, as we both sat Indian-style next to each other, and I noticed that we were in flow, groovin' in a moment of grace that I can't adequately explain. Even though I didn't know it at the time, that's when I first grew to love her, as much as I loved any of my closest friends. From then on, I allowed myself to grow closer to her, a jumbled affection of the physical, mental, emotional and the spiritual. It got to a point where if she didn't come by, I missed her, as much as she missed me if she came by and I wasn't there. During that period, we were best friends. Although I was always aware of the obvious differences, we connected on so many levels that those differences didn't matter.

Keep this in mind as you picture us at the campus bar months later. As I walked back and forth between gettin' food and beer for us, she noticed that amongst a table of three white boys, one of them stared at me with hate in his eyes, glaring angrily between her and me. As I sat down with my back to him, he continued to stare. I didn't have to turn around to see this. I could tell by the uncomfortable look in her eyes. It got so bad she wanted to leave.

As we walked across campus arm in arm, two cars of students drove by, mostly white boys. They pointed at us excitedly, like they just saw a fucking car accident. She asked, "What the hell's wrong with them?" A lot of white girls in that situation react with the same innocent naiveté. I didn't have it in me to explain to her that the sight of a beautiful blonde and a handsome black man short-circuits a lot of minds out there. It's that image held-over from slavery days, Mandigo and Massa's lady. It's titillating to some and revolting to others. Either way, it breeds a reaction that confirms how we're still stuck in the effects of racism.

My relationship with Amber was in stark contrast to one I had with Angela, a sista who, in her own right, was good to go and was available. Physical attractiveness was not an issue; it was her mouth that killed it for me. We couldn't have a conversation without her sayin' "White people this" and "white people that." Believe me; I knew where she was comin' from. I dealt with it every day the same as she did, maybe even more intensely since I didn't have the luxury of separating from the kids I had to work for and with. But with her, it became a constant distraction, like her inability to move beyond what she felt were limitations placed on her by others defined who she was. The negativity that oozed out of her, I felt, was poison. It may have been a snap judgment, right or wrong, but I decided that I didn't want to get close to her. I mean, really, who wants to be around people like that, black or white?

I could've been more proactive in trying to reach out to her, lend more support, or otherwise breach that wall that separates many black men and woman. But in widening the scope a little, I had great friendships with other black women on campus, again, most of whom had boyfriends. Hmm… is there perhaps a connection between feeling good about yourself, or being emotionally settled, and finding it easier to establish connections with other people? I'm throwin' sociological theories out the window on this one. People either click or they don't. Angela and I just didn't click. That distance later became more obvious, exasperated by many situations where I know she saw me eating lunch, or other wise associated, with white people, particularly white girls.

The situation came to a head one day when I made a nasty joke with a mutual acquaintance of ours, another black woman. It had somethin' to do with me jumpin' her bones. She had a boyfriend, and I didn't want to diss him or her, so after I made the joke, I said, "Nah, I'm just playing. You know I wouldn't go after you like that," the implication being that I wasn't down wit' OPP.

Ever been in a situation where you say something, not intending for it to come out the way it did, but knowin' that it'll get twisted? Well, as soon as I said that, I knew somethin' was comin'. Angela whispered something smart in our friend's ear. There were at least two other black people there who heard what she said, like "Oh, girl…No you didn't just say that." I knew it had somethin' to do with me and white girls, but she wouldn't repeat it. I dared her to. I wanted her to, but she wouldn't. This black dude we were with said, "Man, you better just walk on," like

I wasn't ready to go there. Fuck that! I was ready, and I kept daring her to repeat what she said, but she wouldn't. With no resolution in sight, finally, she shouted, "Men suck!"

It was the first time that I was in a situation where I was directly confronted with the ire of a black woman who felt dissed. I have no idea what I would've said to her, actually. What could I possibly say? Stop hatin'? Stop bein' jealous? In any case of perceived rejection, those would be reasonable answers. And it's not as simple as "I like white girls over you." But is it possible to reasonably explain that in an intense situation, especially when someone has already got it made up in their mind that truth only goes as far as what they can see?

There is, undeniably, a wall between black men and black women, and an equally undeniable, funky relationship between black men and white women. It's something a lot of people either don't want to recognize, don't want to talk about, or flat out deny, but it's there. I've always known it, since that summer I spent in Massachusetts between seventh and eighth grade, when this little white girl, Amy, out of nowhere, was all over my shit. But I never had the proper social and historical vocabulary to paint the picture of context outside of my own experiences.

It wasn't until after grad school that I began to understand the dynamics behind these complexities. Casually browsing through Barnes and Noble one day, I came across a book that deals openly with these uncomfortable issues. It was Calvin C. Hernton's *Sex and Racism*, written in the 1960s but still very applicable today. In very plain language, he lays out why we're so fucked up when it comes to racism and its effects. But you don't have to be a historian or a psychologist to figure this shit out. All it takes is a little bit of common sense and knowledge of America's roots.

Slavery fucked us up. And I don't mean just African-Americans. It fucked up all Americans. We haven't gotten past it. Thirty years of civil rights have more blacks and whites working together, going to school together, taking dumps next to each other, and eating next to each other at McDonald's, but in our personal lives, we might as well live on different planets. We're programmed to have distorted notions of each other. We can't help it. It's embedded in the fabric of America as sure as God and capitalism. As black Americans, we may not have heavy irons on our necks, wrists, and ankles, but in a lot of ways, there still exists that master/slave relationship between blacks and whites, and it affects all relationships in general: black and white, male and female, and everything in between.

When I was learning about slavery in school, they talked about brutality and cruelty to slaves, a little bit. White slave-owning men perpetuated stereotypes about blacks in order to justify the enslavement and abuse of other human beings. In order to make blacks seem less than human, all kinds of shit was attached to us: we're three-fifths human, uncivilized, fit for heavy labor, happy to be in bondage, etc. But there was this other shit goin' on that was sexually charged. Black men and women are supposed to be sexual beasts of primal fear/lust.

This, of course, led to the widespread rape of black women by white slave-owners and the subsequent lynching and castrations of black men during and after slavery, much of the time surrounding accusations of raping white women. These aren't exactly secrets, but the psychology behind these associations isn't necessarily acknowledged. While white slave owners were raping or otherwise forcing sex from their female slaves, depriving black women of their womanhood, their wives saw their husbands slippin' down to the quarters every night, seemingly more sexually attracted to the Africans than to them. At the same time, their female slaves were birthing light-skinned, kinky-haired babies while the wives are constantly being told that their virtue and perfect picture of womanhood had to be protected from the dangerous Negro man. Black men had the stigma of being a threat to white women thrust upon us, and we were powerless to protect our own women.

In the minds of the slave-owners, their rational was that if they couldn't control their lust for black women, people who supposedly weren't quite human, wouldn't black men want to do the same with white women? They couldn't have that, so everything within their power, from law to severe social taboo, was put into place to prevent black men and white women from any kind of sexual contact. It was their irrational fear, born out of their own guilt for being rapists and liking it, that inadvertently created the undeniable tension we see today between white women and black men, fear rooted in hypocrisy and sexual perversion.

Meanwhile, what do you think the wives of slave-owners were thinkin' as their husbands crawled back into their beds in the wee hours of the morning after a jaunt down to the slave quarters? And could those thoughts have been similar to those of the male slaves, the ones who were told they would lose their cocks and/or their lives if they ever thought of looking at a white woman? What do you think happens after years and years of that shit?

The birth of what we now call Jungle Fever, American style, peppered with the Euro-Christian suppression of sexual expression inherit in the culture.

Please understand something. I'm not sayin' that *all* white women want Mandingo, or *all* white dudes wanna dip their peanut butter in chocolate, or vice-versa. It's much more complicated than that. For sure, if the Southern white woman thought about getting back at her slave-owning husband by fuckin' a buck, it was just as much of a power grab over an object that was powerless as it was fulfillment of curiosity; a reaffirmation of the womanhood that was taken away from her by the myth that she was too perfect and pure to be fucked the way any woman wants lovin'.

That's the tragic legacy of slavery that few are unwilling to confront. It dehumanized everybody. It was the beginning of the wall that separates black men and women, mentally and emotionally shackling black men with a sense of powerlessness. Further, it internalized a sense of frustration in black women aimed at black men for being powerless. It also continued in the social and psychological effects of institutionalized, government-sanctioned segregation. White women, already second-class citizens, were propelled to a mythic status, without real dignity and respect, which they could never live up to, further shackling any real sense of being female and human. Finally, the power structure of this country, dominated by white men, rooted itself in hypocrisy, where delusion and lies became a mode of survival for those in control. The humanity of black people couldn't be acknowledged, for the wealth of this nation depended on us not being human, i.e. slaves. Hence, to take away the humanity of another is to deprive oneself of their own, for then the oppressor, in continuing the lie, lives in schizophrenic denial of truth, perhaps even reaching a point where the lies become truth.

These psychological relationships underlie our social conceptions of each other, whether it be unmentioned, unacknowledged attraction buried under taboo, unhealthy obsession based on stereotypes, revulsion based irrational prejudice, or the twisted tension that's created by all of the above. What started as myths underlie how we view one another.

'What the fuck, Ron? You sayin' all black/white couples got the fever?'

No, but it's there. I believe, like any bleeding heart, idealistic dreamer, that people can connect regardless of who they are or where they come from, as rare as that may actually happen. But when you see a black/white couple, more often than not, it's a black man and a white woman, the more extreme taboo of the white/black, male/female dynamic. Just the fact that the taboo exists adds an air of excitement and juiciness to any interracial possibility. We're more relaxed about it now than we've ever been, but it's still a hang-up in the consciousness of America.

Even if blacks and whites connect mostly on the fever level: so what? What's wrong with curiosity? God forbid we might actually come to see each other as human beings. Then again, the sexualization of racism is an inherent part of the problem to begin with. But is it better for blacks and whites to study each other's humanity from afar than to deny the most base level of the black/white connection: sexual attraction/revulsion?

The separation of identity between blacks and whites only adds to the confusion beneath our perceptions of each other, whether it's guilt for breaking taboos or obsession with imbedded images, further tarnishing whatever good can come from interracial relationships. Anything can be an unhealthy obsession. What makes interracial relations seem unhealthy is the fact that we make it seem like sin. Considering the history of black/white relationships in this country, it's understandable. People don't want to fess up to the mess that racism created between us and within us. More importantly, people don't wanna fess up to their own personal inadequacies concerning the issue.

That angry white dude in the bar, the one scopin' Amber and I: what the fuck was goin' on in his mind? It was the sight of she and I together that fucked with his head. She wasn't a black-cock lover, but he could only imagine us rumblin' in the jungle. Who's really got the fever here? Did the Fever underlie our relationship? I don't doubt it, but it didn't matter. We loved each other as people first and foremost. That didn't matter to him. He hated her, himself, and me. But it was too much for him to deal with the inadequacy goin' on in his own head. I was spendin' time with a beautiful blonde, and he was hangin' with his sausage party. The jealousy inherent in that situation isn't anything unusual, but the fact that I was black no doubt exasperated it. The hatred started from within him. There was something about himself he hated, but it was easier to take it out on us.

And then there's Angela and all the black women who feel betrayed, abandoned, and *unattractive*. Actually, it's not just black woman. Considering all the shit that happened during and after slavery, it's the black-politically correct thing to *not* have romantic associations with whites. Friends, co-workers, happy hour buddies: that's cool. Hell, you can even have 'em over for some soul food. But as lovers?

For many African-Americans, the political reason why we *shouldn't* "mix" is because we need a "strong, black nation." The availability of black men becomes an issue, considering that we're incarcerated at depressing rates compared to all others in America.

I don't know about you, but when I go out, I *always* see single, available black men, but that's beside the point. The real issue here is this: how far does social obligation intrude into the personal spheres of our lives? Social responsibility is, no doubt, important. And whether we want it to be so or not, just about everything we do is influenced by the politics of our culture. But how much should those politics dictate love or lust? How much do our own personal experiences, thoughts, and choices influence what happens in our individual lives? It's something that everyone, regardless of political, racial, or social standing, has to deal with on an individual level.

And that is the crux of any discussion pertaining to race and sex, or anything else for that matter: personal choices. Everybody's looking for love, or their version of it. If somebody's havin' a hard time finding a mate, sometimes you have to just call it what it is: a personal problem. If you walk around bitter, spiteful and angry, no matter what your color or gender, of course nobody's gonna want to be with yo' ass, except maybe somebody else who's equally as bitter, spiteful and angry. Self-esteem and happiness aren't things that anyone else can give you. Having gone through unrelenting droughts of loneliness, I know this. Obtaining that image of "the perfect mate," whether it be an image that fits a politically correct ideal, or some acceptable, social construct, or a sincere belief in knowing what you want, ain't gonna essentially change who you are or how you feel about yourself. So blaming interracial couples for taking away potential mates skirts the point of personal responsibility. If not that, it's just an easy excuse to put others down for not following the rules, reaffirming a sense of group identity to compensate for the insecurity that comes with being an individual and having your own thoughts.

I know all too well the frustrations of black women. But as somebody who has no problem crossing the lines, what kind of adequate explanation am I gonna give for why I think the way I do? Have I given in to the beauty myth created around white women? Am I ashamed of my black self, my people?

I'll tell you what: I *love* being black. I love my chocolate-coated bald head. But just like everybody else, I grew up watchin' television, and the viral media infected me to a degree. I'd love to tell you my early media crushes were glamorous black women, but they weren't. It was Brook Shields in *The Blue Lagoon*. Janet from *Three's Company*. The red-head from *Hart to Hart*.

Then again, I loved Thelma from *Good Times*, and Janet Jackson's beautiful, 13-year-old ass, and that one black dancer from *Solid Gold*. See? I wasn't totally brainwashed. Is it possible that a guy like me just appreciates beauty in its varying forms?

But I understand how, at times, black women are annoyed by white girls and black dudes together, because a lot of the time it *does* stem from stereotypes, particularly from the white girl's point of view. After all, black men aren't different than any other man who easily arouses at the sight of a beautiful woman. Not to put it all off on the white girls, but it's somethin' else when they aggressively pursue black dudes. Maybe it's a double standard, but, fuck it; I'm a guy. What do you want from me?

I can illustrate a typical case of what I'm talkin' about. I stayed up at Fairfield's campus the summer after graduation and met this white girl, Lisa, a non-practicing Jew. I got to know her through a mutual friend. I'd seen her around a few times with her hip-hop, inner-city style. She stood out on that campus at that time. The first night we talked, she revealed a lot of things about herself: a traumatic first sexual encounter (with a white dude), a string of unhealthy relationships after that, strain and separation from her folks, a stint as an under-aged stripper in New York, and a catalogue of boyfriends, including a Jamaican drug dealer.

The thing I liked most about her was her eclectic taste in literature, like eastern philosophy-type shit. Of course, she was also strictly hip-hop and R&B in dress, manner, and talk, almost to the point of hilarity, a true wiggerette. The thing that killed me the most about her was her favorite activity: going down to the outdoor basketball courts on campus to check out the brothas who came over from Bridgeport, the hood next to Fairfield. She likened herself to Susan Sarandon's character from "Bull Durham" who adopted a ball player, every season, to bang and nurture.

I tried to give her the benefit of the doubt because she was mostly cool, but one night, I caught her in the middle of a conversation, "Like...totally talking like...this white girl, from like...the middle of Suburbia... Ohmigod!" But she swore to me that white guys didn't do anything for her. White *people* pissed her off. She swore allegiance to black culture, would only "date" black men, and she admitted, in the middle of a heated discussion, "I just like to get fucked!"

All right, I'll admit it... I didn't have the confidence at that time to knock that ass out the box, although I'm not so sure I wanted to anyway. She easily out-weighed me by some decent poundage. And so many guys, by her own admission, ran up through her, it intimidated me. After all, I'm not Long Dong Silver, and I actually had a feelin' that I wouldn't meet her expectations.

Maybe I was better off. I don't regret not fuckin' her. I was actually proud that I didn't give in to that Fever thing so easily. I examined her intentions and mine more carefully than I ever did with a white girl before then. I didn't want to be Joe Black, down with the Any-of-Them-Will-Do Crew. I couldn't get past her "Black" act and her slutiness. Plus, I caught a peek at the gap between her legs when she was wearin' a bikini. It was was wider than the Long Island Sound.

She straight up saw black men as bucks, as symbols, not as people. It's fucked up when a white person thinks that being "black" means sayin' certain things in a certain way, or dressing a certain way, or liking and disliking certain things because that's supposedly the way black people think. She would even go so far as to make fun of me because I liked rock music, callin' me a white boy in front of a black girl this one time. Can you believe that shit?

To me, there's a big difference between being a genuine part of black culture, whether you're black or not growin' up around it, or if you're mimicking that culture. It's like post Civil-Rights minstrelsy: the new Al Jolson, sambo caricature. Underneath the act is the notion that blacks are two-dimensional characters. She thought she was being cool and hip, but she was really being foolish, if not unintentionally racist.

I'd seen cases like her before: white chicks that had some kind of trauma in their past, trauma that fucks with their self-esteem, and as a result, they associate with what's considered the lowest common denominator in American society – "blackness." She, as she saw herself, was not the image of what white people are supposed to live up to, the image of unspoken superiority. Her past was dirty. Also, "blackness" has a titillating, anti-establishment thing about it, promulgated by MTV and the media at large. So it becomes easier for people like her to associate with blacks; the more ghetto, the more uncouth, the more stereotypical, the better. I'm not a psychologist, but I've seen the connections over and over again.

Even if trauma isn't the factor that drives these kinds of chicks to black men, the curiosity factor alone may be enough to do it. So in cases like this, I can see how black women get annoyed by the black/white thing, especially if the man doesn't know what's really goin' on.

I think more than anything, it's the *image* of white women being more desirable to black men that bothers black women. And why wouldn't it? The idea of white beauty is practically stamped on us all. I can see how that makes black women feel unwanted and insecure.

But it's still just an image, and it's up to us as individuals to see beyond it. To internalize the feeling of being unwanted because of the sight of black men with white women defuses personal responsibility and self-power. And it wouldn't matter if a frustrated black woman found the blackest, most perfect black man. Ultimately, that same initial insecurity will play itself out later, and that man will never do enough or be enough to satisfy. And that doesn't just go for black women; anybody who thinks their happiness lies in another person is setting themselves up for the exact opposite. But I think that with some patience, self-awareness and a little luck, we can all get what we need out of life, whether it be a mate that's good for us or all those other things we whine to God about.

It's the hold-over images from slavery that are the real destructive forces that keep us from understanding the truth of our collective humanity. The mere sight of a black man walking or talking with a white woman bothers a lot of people, whether they're sexually involved or not. There's somethin' wrong with *that*, not with the couple, assuming that they are a couple. Even if they are, they aren't actually doing anything wrong to anyone, other than perhaps themselves. When somebody freaks out at the sight of an interracial couple, doesn't that really mean there's something wrong within that person? It fucks with their perceptions on how things should be. The viewer is experiencing themselves through the couple, a confusion of contradictory feelings: revulsion, to legitimize what we're taught about how wrong mixing is, or curiosity, however subtle, which then brings fear, however subtle, of breaking the rules, a self-diagnostic of whether or not we would, could, or should satisfy that curiosity. Inside peoples' heads is where the real shit happens. How 'bout some mass group therapy here!

But what are you gonna do when people don't want to own up to their own demons? Do you give in to the idea of racial purity, whether it's a reaction to racism from another group, or racism from within your own? Are cultural loyalty and social duty the end-all and be-all to one's heritage and existence? Even if one feels a genuine obligation for sticking with their own, who are they, or you or I, to impose our personal beliefs on others? We're not talkin' about murder.

Most people feel obligated not to succumb to any urge, however minute, to break severe taboos. But it's the sheer absoluteness of taboo that creates an inevitable tension to break it. We all share this tension. It connects and separates us, leaving us to walk around like the crazy schizophrenics we are.

Who knows what the circumstances are that bring people together in union: blacks, whites, and everyone in-between? It could be curiosity, fascination, or whatever. God forbid the idea that *some* people can actually see others for who they are and not what they're supposed to be. Stereotyped images from clouded minds are real the sources of the problem, not race-mixing. Is it really so bad when two people who don't look alike, who come from different cultures, want to be with each other? Does it automatically mean that they're victims of taboo, inextricably drawn to each other out of some perverse curiosity, or brainwashed by the ideals of the dominant culture? Maybe. But we're not talkin' about cats and dogs, apples and oranges. We're talkin' about *people*.

The Fever is in me, no doubt. I'm not innocent of my own inherent rebellious nature, which draws me more toward anything considered taboo, sometimes detrimentally. And I won't bother with excuses. We are who we are, and we do the best we can given our awareness at the time. Even so, it hurts me that people hurt from these fucked up images of "race" embedded in our American minds. There is no easy solution to any of these problematic issues. Dare I imagine that we can one day get to a point where this discussion is moot?

The best we can hope to do is understand, accept and deal with the cards we were given. I'd love to be the idealist and hope that some cataclysmic event will shake down the barriers that keep us from acknowledging our humanity. But it's gonna be damned hard, and I don't see it in the foreseeable future.

Until then, long live curiosity. It just helps to understand the things behind it.

I've spent so much time, energy, and anxiety caught between black and white that I got to a point where I realized… everybody's fucked up. Just finding someone; a friend, a casual date, or a lover, who's halfway as sane as you are, is blessing enough rather than worrying about how different they look than you. It seems like I've always lived outside the bubble like that. I don't know if it was a conscious choice or just part of who I've always been, but I choose to thrive on it now because more often than not, those inside the bubble, who live their lives like sheep, thoughtlessly following the cues of others, are more fucked up than those of us outside the bubble. Too many people limit themselves, not just in choosing potential mates, but in general 'cuz they're worried about what others will think of them. It's easier to figure out who you are when you don't worry about that and stay true to yourself.

This race/relationship thing played a significant part in me figuring myself out, as a human being, as a man, as an African-American character in this mad game. How we view race and sex in America is a barometer of true freedom, freedom that has to start from within. I learned more about accepting myself as going against the grain, tight-roping on the rims of my own ideology. It's made it easier for me to grapple with that question mark in my head, working from some semblance of self identity.

I choose to erase that line that separates us, erasing a line within myself at the same time, and I accept the ire of those who fall short of the idea that it's all good: black, white, and everything in-between. I accept it without feeling bad about it. I can't help or change people's limitations. Or rather, I'm not really tryin' to. The problem's too big, and it was one of the roadblocks that kept me from that thing I was lookin' for.

To Be or Bu-Jee

Alan relayed a story to me about trying to hail a cab for fifteen to twenty minutes on a cold Chicago evening, getting passed repeatedly only to see cabs stop for white passengers a block away. When he finally did hail down a taxi, in frustration, he told the driver about what had just happened to him.

Lots of people would simply shrug off a story like that, like this obviously paranoid, delusional black man is only looking for sympathy, for surely things like that only happen in the minds of thousands of African-American men. This cabby, who was Middle-Eastern, sympathized with Alan. He said, "I just want you to know that black people are just as good as white people."

Um…yeah. Thanks.

The driver had good intentions, but think about that for a second. If he placed white people on the pedestal as being the norm, or what's considered to be "as good as," then what does that say about his feelings toward his own ethnicity? Is he right up there with white folks? Is he just beneath them? Maybe he thought that both blacks and whites are actually *beneath* him. Who knows?

I don't know where that cab driver was comin' from, but this story illustrates how the separation of blacks and whites and all others in between play out in subtleties, from the way we think to the things we say. I'm just as much infected with the mess of race as anybody, for this is the legacy we've all inherited here in America. But when you're black, it's something you're forced to think about 24-7, from when you're followed around a clothing store to when a woman crosses the street when she sees you coming her way, even if she's black. You can't help but question whether there's any escape from how perceptions shape your very existence, or if there's any possibility of shaping and maintaining an identity beyond those perceptions; the perception of what it means to be black.

Alan

"This is something that I've learned to do. In Atlanta – I never really noticed this in Chicago, but I'm sure it happens all the time – when I was in Atlanta, though, I noticed that when I went into stores, there was a noticeable difference in the way I was treated. Not necessarily the following-me-around-the-store syndrome, but other stuff, like, 'Hello. How are you.' That's what they gave white people. With a black person, when you come in, you'll be lucky if they say anything to you, or it'll be like a subdued, 'Hi.' Totally rigid: a different treatment altogether. Sometimes it's just flat out rude.

"One time, I went into this Wal-Mart kind of place. I used to always see this guy who worked there. He was kinda slow. He had a speech impediment. He was at the magazine rack, which was right near the register He noticed me coming up, so he looped around to the next cash register. I was walking up, not really paying attention. Apparently, there was a sign that said, 'Next Register Please.' He said, 'That register's closed.' Then under his breath he said, 'If you read the sign, you would've seen that.'

"I said, 'Excuse me, what did you say?' He repeated it. He was bold enough to repeat it! I said, 'Don't you dare talk down to me.' I guess he was used to shiftless Negroes just kind of bumbling around like, 'Oh, my fault, man. I didn't see the sign.' What was I supposed to do, join in and laugh at myself for his ridiculing me?

"When he saw that I stood up for myself, that I wouldn't take his rudeness, he immediately cowered. 'Oh no, no! I wasn't trying to talk down to you. I wasn't saying that at all.' He totally back peddled. They switch from being an arrogant asshole to wanting to bend over backwards for you. The thing is; why would you think that's an okay thing to say to somebody anyway, regardless of looks or intelligence? I know where people are coming from. I empathize, but they're not gonna to take your shit out on me, nor should they take it out on anyone.

"I always think the easy way out is to get mad about it. The better way is to try and make them look like the fools they are. I waited for him to count my change up. As he handed it to me, I said, 'It's not my fault you're a cash register clerk.' Then I just turned around and walked away. I heard him slam the register. That motherfucka was pissed! I had to make him feel as bad as he made me feel.

"I got good about that when I was working at this restaurant. I had a mastery of the English language that most of the waiters there didn't. A lot of times, when I felt that people were condescending to me, I would condescend right back to them in a way that just pissed them off even more. But I wouldn't get upset. I'd do it with a smile. There's no way to sting them harder than that. When you beat them at the word game, they're pissed. You're making them look dumb. There's nothing worse than ignorant hate than to be made to look ignorant in the eyes of those they assume to be ignorant or genetically inferior. So that's what I try to do. If I allow them to get a rise out of me, that's what they want, because they already think we have tempers anyway and fly off the handle at the drop of a dime.

"I'm not gonna sweat shit like that. It's not worth sweating, but it's fucked up.

It's that little subtle thing."

"When I was waiting tables, I really got a window into [race] shit. This restaurant I worked in wasn't really upper crust. We attracted a lot of middle class people, black and white. It just so happens that the blacks that came in... More often than not, the troublemakers were black. It was so fucked up. [They were] always looking to get over on the restaurant. It incensed me to the utmost because I would actually see servers arguing about whether or not they would wait on a black table. That shit happens all the time.

"They dreaded Freaknik (a yearly gathering of black Greek fraternities and sororities). Nobody was looking forward to it. The atmosphere was really uncomfortable, and it wasn't like anybody could say anything. I'm sure they probably said shit when I wasn't around, but people, for the most part, tried to be politically correct, as politically correct as you can be about being racist.

"And it's weird because I was a waiter too, and I could empathize because I know that black folks generally don't tip as well: lower class or middle class. It's not even just strictly about class because the bourgeois blacks were sometimes worse than the lower-class blacks. They would pitch a bitch at anything. It's like when they came in, they had this expectation. It might even be subconscious, where we're expecting foul treatment. We're so used to our daily frustrations in the white world that when we come into a restaurant, it's one of the few times where it is MANDATORY that we're bossing somebody around, like, 'You gotta do what I say.'

"So we take advantage of that. We totally revel in the fact that we got this server. So a lot of us take it to the extreme. 'I don't like this, take this back to the cook.' Or we'll eat 3/4 of a steak and say, 'I didn't like this. It was undercooked. I'm not paying for this.' I can go on at length. I've seen situations where the manager takes plates, orders a whole other round of food for the table, and then comps the meal. And on top of that, the folks are upset that they didn't get the proper service. I guess there's this little known fact that if you complain for any reason, they'll give you your meal for free. And people just do it.

"They'll run you around, but they won't tip you. They'll take it out on you. They're looking for any one thing, any flaw in your service, so they'll have an excuse not to tip you. That's what leads to servers not wanting to wait on black folks. Even the manager realizes it, so the waiters don't get in trouble. It's like a downward spiral.

"I can't tell you how many times in a given night black folks would find the manager and complain about something. It becomes, like, crying wolf. Eventually, it'll get to a point where our complaints are falling on deaf ears. It's like the chicken or the egg. I don't know where it starts first. Obviously, blacks are used to not getting good service in general. So we're reacting in a sense. But us reacting contributes to us continuing to not get good service. White people get defensive because they say, 'Oh, here's another attitudinal black table, so I'm immediately going to put my defenses up and be rigid when I'm dealing with them.' We sense that, and then we say, 'That server was rude to me. Where's the manager?'

"To this day it's a sore spot because when I go out with my black friends, they start talking that talk. 'Hmmph. That server didn't get here in 2.5 minutes. We *know where his tip is going.' That shit gets me incensed, and these are my friends. I'm like, 'Look, I know the pain. I'm there with you, but it's got to stop somewhere!'*

"I look at my waiter experience, like anything, as a microcosm of the real problem on the outside. If we don't take responsibility for our own actions and wrongdoings, then we can't blame white folks for reacting. Granted, we're both to blame for reacting, and they are to blame more so than blacks for past wrongdoings, but we have to take responsibility for our own actions. If you're going to walk into a restaurant knowing that you're going to pitch a bitch, don't get mad when you get bad service in the future. Pitching a bitch doesn't make anything better. It makes things worse, and you get bad service. It builds up. We don't see the big picture. It's like we're all little parts from a cookie cutter. You are a little isolated incident that is a carbon copy of what happens all the time, everywhere. If you can understand that, you might be able to make a little more sense of it.

"It's fucked up. So when I walk into a restaurant now and get fucked up service, I know where it's coming from, but at the same time I'm placed in an awkward position because I don't know what to do. It's like, fuck! Well, they are being rude, and I'm being chill about it, but what do I do? Do I overcompensate with the tip to show that I understand their situation?

"'(In a Buckwheat voice) I'm not like them bad niggas you used to waiting on.'

"Or do I tip them according to the rude service, which confirms their rudeness to me? It's a weird thing I'll never be able to resolve."

"I still have... I don't know if I'll ever get over this. It's happened more since college, where I feel... I'm so sick that I meet fellow black people, and they assume certain things about me because I'm not, like, 'black enough.' That shit pisses me off. I'm really defensive about it.

"Georgetown was a lot like that for me, too. So I'm like, 'If y'all are gonna go ahead and assume that I'm this wannabe white motherfucka, then I might as well just go ahead and... You're punishing me from the black community in a sense, so why am I gonna continue to fight you to accept me, while you have these other motherfuckas over here; they could care less. They're not hung up by that bullshit.' Naturally, I'm gonna hang out with people who ain't gonna give a shit about the way I talk, or the interests I have, or the music I listen to. Why should I fight y'all to want to be down with y'all? That's bullshit.

"In some ways, it almost seems purposeful, and I'm sure at some point it was, that if you give certain black people opportunities and deprive those opportunities from others, then you're immediately going to cause a rift in that community, and it's divide and conquer. The blacks who have opportunities will be so happy that they've got this newfound material splendor that they're going to do everything within their power to hold onto it and distance themselves from the lower classes that don't have any of that shit.

"And we all know that once black people – even if they wanted to go back to their communities and try to have that trickle down effect – they won't be accepted by the lower classes. It's an inevitable rift. It's fucked up. What pisses me off, when I come to my people with open arms, I feel like they're shunning me, and it's *just like, 'Damn! If we worked together, we would be so powerful.' But they're so insecure about our situation that they diss me.*

"And there's plenty of black folk out there like that. You know, bourgeois folks who think that they're too good for you. But I'M not like that, and I feel like you're punishing me for trying to be down, so I don't try anymore. It's a weird sort of thing.

"They have this thing called 'First Fridays' in Chicago. It's very prevalent in the summer time. 'First Fridays' is like a networking thing for black people. It starts as a cocktail party after work and then there are after parties at various clubs. At around 11:00 at night, you'll see all these various black folks running around with their suits on. I'm thinking to myself, '11:00 at night. What the fuck do you need a suit on for? Did you come right from work, or did you go home and get changed into a suit, and come back out?' Mostly, people don't need a suit to begin with at work. They just wear suits strictly to show that they got some kind of game going on. The whole thing is just so damn DISGUSTING to me. It just makes me want to fucking vomit. Why do we have to go so far out of our way to profile like that? And this is the middle class, the so-called 'Talented Tenth' we're talking about here.

"The circle of friends that I have been blessed to meet represents a group of blacks that I find so hard to come into contact with – not the ones who are strictly hip-hop generation, not the ones who are bourgeois beyond belief, but the ones who can appreciate different things, have varied interests, and are not pretentious or concerned about showing off material wealth. It's so good. It's so refreshing to be around them.

"It just depresses me that we lack vision outside of our little enclave. And again, of course it's justified in a sense that we live in a world that's always telling us that we're not okay, so we're reacting. We want to stick to our little group and keep our blinders on because we're trying to soak up our shit. It is justified, but nonetheless, it's still disturbing.

"That's why I have a tough time with the whole dating scene. I know I'm not going to find the person I want to marry in one of those bourgeois First Friday events. I would love nothing more than to marry a black woman that I was totally cool with. In corporate America, I see black women who are very forceful and authoritative. They go out of their way to be way bossy. My friend was telling me about this girl who he was working underneath. They sort of over-compensate being marginalized by being these super-bossy, authoritative types that no one really likes anyway because they're so, 'I'm the shit.' I don't like hearing that kind of shit because it's self-importance.

"That's what it is, and that's what happens to these bourgeois folks. They get into these self-important mindsets where they're mightier than thou because they have a college education, or maybe a grad school education and they've got such and such jobs. Therefore, they are automatically worthy of people just giving them the utmost respect. That's white or black.

"So when they come into restaurants, they want...no, they DEMAND respect. It's self-importance, and to me, that's sin. I'm sure there's somewhere in the Bible that says this is wrong because it's like saying you're mightier than God is, or on

the same level as God. That just bums me out to the utmost. They're like, 'I am so important that I have to have these gadgets, and people need to get in touch with me, and I need to have these nice cars, and these little material goods to show you that I'm important.' It's like idolatry. That's exactly what it is.

"KRS-One had a song about love. People's love is really of their material goods and not of one another. If anything, I try to combat that. I don't want to seem like I'm too...stylish. I like clothes a lot. I've always been very fashion conscious, but over the last few years, I've toned that down because I don't want to appear like I'm one of these over-stylish folk out there just thinking they're the shit. I think its bullshit that we have these badges.

"If anything, once you graduate, it can become even more of a badge that people show around, with their little fraternity/sorority license plates. It's like, 'Damn y'all!' We always gotta be showing off some shit. It's, '(A) I went to college (B) I was about some shit when I was in college.' You see 'Alpha' and that automatically makes a statement to people. I totally understand where it comes from.

"There's class-ism that exists in the black community; middle class and lower class. Obviously, everybody wants to been seen as middle class by way of cellular phone, or Versace suits, sorority key chains, or whatever. These are all idols that people hold up to validate themselves, like, 'Hey, I'm an important person!' I never subscribed to that shit. I see that as weakness, and I never want to be around anybody who's so insecure that they need idols to validate themselves. That's just fucking bullshit to me. I'll never tolerate that.

"At least I can catch myself in my bourgeois-ness. I see how we're divided by social classes within the confines of race. We all fall into moments of lapse, but you gotta keep catchin' yourself, always reminding yourself about these things or else you will become bourgeois before you know it.

"This story illustrates this best. We went to this function for Roland Burris. He's a black politician here in Chicago. They were counting the votes up. It was Mike, Erin, and I. We're sittin' in the corner saying, 'Look at this. This is the biggest, bourgeois bullshit I've ever seen. People all up in here with their wine, talking all foo-foo, I can't fuckin' believe we're here. I'm sick just lookin at this.' There were disses back and forth talking about these motherfuckas.

"So then this dude comes up to us. He's got his collar all fucked up, his tie is askew, and he was like, 'Uh, say brotha, uh, did you find out the score of the Bull's game tonight?'

"So Mike was like, 'Ah, no, didn't quite catch that. Sorry, mmkay?' And we went back to our conversation.

"Oh my god! And if it wasn't for me pointing that out... 'Y'all don't realize what just happened, do you? You don't even know what we just did. Here we are dissin' all these bourgeois motherfuckas in the room, and this brotha asks us for a sports score, and we don't wanna have the time of day. We don't wanna be seen next to this muhfucka!' We started dying laughing 'cuz we knew how fucked up we were.

"Erin reminds us of that all the time whenever Mike and I get into our little rant sessions on the hip-hoppers. 'Think about that poor brotha who asked you for

the Bulls score and you didn't even want to talk with him!'

"It was so typical. That encapsulated the problem right there: we don't want to admit our own fallacies. We're too afraid to expose ourselves in the mirror. That moment could have passed, and no one would've said shit, and we would have forgotten about it. Goddamn!

"You gotta stay on top of shit. You gotta keep reminding yourself, you know what I'm saying? We're taught to act this way. We're conditioned *to act these ways. That doesn't mean that we have to accept it."*

What, exactly, does it mean to be black? Does it mean having skin anywhere along the color spectrum of off-white to charcoal? Does it mean talkin' with a little twang? Does it mean finger-lickin' chicken and collard greens, dancin' to the drummers beat, jumpin' high and runnin' fast with dicks draggin' in the dirt?

Generally, the idea of being "black" in America originally served to validate an idea that the ruling class, made up of "whites," had a right to consider us as their polar opposite: inferior and not worthy of humanity; to be kept down, kept away, in the back if at all, separated, and despised for purposes originating in the desire for free labor. We are the walking embodiment of America's sense of moral failure and inadequacy, the mirror of hypocrisy in lieu of "All men are created equal." Things may have changed a bit since Civil Rights, but for the most part, blacks are more tolerated than really accepted as equals, the inevitable legacy of what was a brand of apartheid.

A sincere governmental desire, driven by people who care about racism, to have something like a truth and reconciliation panel would go a great way toward bridging that gap between blacks and whites set in motion with the birth of this country. We need to put our shit on the table in order to move forward, despite the claim of what a conservative would call historical revisionism.

But, honestly, it's not at all certain that America will ever reach that level of thought and desire. Not that normal people wouldn't go for something sensible, but this country's focus isn't allowed to go in that direction, detoured by old prejudices lived out in current experiences, mistrust and misunderstanding between blacks and whites (encouraged by The Few who profit from the separation of people who don't see their real common enemy), and constant misdirection about the truth of the shameful parts of America's history. Until some cataclysmic disturbance in the status quo changes these things, we'll still play the race game, where definitions of black and white, whether people consciously think about these things or not, become issues in shaping identity, both personally and nationally.

The fact that we still use the terms black and white says it all, for these terms don't imply color or ethnicity as much as they imply a whole set of notions we often take for granted, including an inferior/superior relationship. These notions were handed to us, and because the game is still tight, they play themselves out based on what we've been taught. It is possible to rise above these archaic, stifling terms. Shit, I think it's essential to any possibility of hope for the future of everyone in this country, because if that ever occurs, it would inherently come with the opening of many other doors, most of which could point us to what's really important in this world and in life, beyond the pod existence of a consumer culture that's destroying a lot more than our personal identities.

But this question of blackness was inevitably a forefront issue for Alan and me. Right around the time we were in school in the 80s and 90s, during the resurgence of Afro-centrism, everything was about blackness. Black to the future. Spike Lee movies. African Studies majors. The Red, the Black, and the Green. It was all good, but somewhere in the middle was the concept of "blackness." What does it mean to be black? Who sets the standard here? Who's blacker than thou?

The "African" in African-American is something distant to look back on and say, "We were more than just slaves." I can dig the idea of roots, but here and now, we are definitely more American than African, with all the history that goes with it. And like America itself, we can mutate and go off in all kinds of different directions and ideas about who we are. There's still this entity called "The Black Community," an amalgamation of identity based on shared experiences, i.e. white racism, but there are whole communities within that community. Is it fair to say that someone can be more black than another?

I get a kick out of the hints of truth I hear when black comedians make fun of guys like O.J. Simpson and Clarence Thomas. But then I think about a guy like Chris Darden, one of the prosecutors in the Simpson trial, who had the weight of black America on his ass because defense attorney Johnny "Cock-stud" Cochran played up these notions of "blackness" in order to get a killer off the hook (for those of you still in denial, sorry, but O.J. did it). Darden was made to look like the sellout black man who was being used by The System in order to put another black man in jail. The truth was that Darden was doing what any decent human being would do in that situation: his job, a job based on justice and truth. No doubt, Cochran was doin' his job, too, but who was the real sellout here: someone trying to get justice, someone trying to win by any means necessary, or someone who sold their soul a long time ago? All those people who cheered at the not-guilty verdict couldn't or wouldn't see through the bullshit laid over their eyes by the notions of race and "blackness."

So again, what does blackness really mean?

The meanings that we have attached to blackness are sometimes purely reactionary. So if whites consider us inferior, we in turn consider them inferior for not having the ability to rise above the delusion of their assumed superiority. So in the name of group identity, truth, including the truth of who we are as human beings, has that much more of a chance to get lost on both sides. Having a comfortable tag often becomes more important than what's real and true.

And maybe that's the blessing that guys like Alan and I can take from our experiences of not quite fitting into any comfortable mode. It becomes easier to recognize and call out bullshit when we see it without feeling the pressure of going against group identification. Of course we still identify ourselves as black, for as any self-aware black person in America knows, the color of our skin gives us no choice. But having significant exposure outside the confines of our race gave us more of a chance to discover that self-identity is made up of so much more than historical and social inevitability.

But the splintering of "black" identity within Alan and me is the downside.

We've been fortunate to have had the opportunities we had, so it's easier for me to tell people in The Hood not to hang onto hate and resentment for past and present wrongdoings by America at large. But then again, whatever I say to my fellow blacks, I wonder if I would be heard? I talk differently than the average brotha where I come from. I dress different. I just *seem* different. It's obvious that I've spent my formative years around whites. I'm confident and, when I want to be, somewhat comfortable around them. A lot of African-Americans are still not. Whether I like it or not, that makes me different and adds to a sense of separation. I'm just as cool bein' around my own, but that feeling of separation is there. I've been told by a few black men that I act conceited, like I'm better than they are. I consciously try not to come off like that despite my tendency to pronounce full sentences in Standard English. I suspect that, a lot of the time, there's resentment that I've had opportunities that many African-Americans still don't get. I've received (arguably) a quality education and I've positioned myself for easier access to social and financial advantages, but unfortunately, in the minds of many black folks, that equates to wanting to be "white." Again, that idea stems from a fatalistic acceptance on the part of black Americans of this country's reluctance to include us totally and unequivocally.

But that's really the point of this all. What *am* I tryin' to achieve? What are we as black people (and all other people) tryin' to achieve?

Mine is a generation of African-Americans who has as good a chance as any to achieve "The American Dream." But my "dream" wasn't really mine. My parents' dream became my dream. The dreams of their generation of kinfolk were their dreams. And then there were the generations of kinfolk before them who could do nothing but dream. And then there's the O.G. of dreams, the "dream" of the Founding Fathers of this country, the wig-wearin' white boys who ran the whole shebang, the dream that generations of black folks were long denied. But what is this dream really all about? Is it about equality among men, working to improve our lives and the lives of others? Or is it about getting good grades, attending prestigious schools, hard work for the company, two cars, 3.5 kids, livin' in the Burbs where every house looks the same, job-hopping, living in debt because we buy things we don't need, or can't afford the things we do need, 401ks, and retirement with a social security system that may not be there in the future? The next thing, the next thing, the next thing. Are we *all* indeed chasing a dream?

By going to school and earning degrees, I achieved what generations of black folks before me couldn't. I was given the opportunity to play the game successfully. I experienced no outer barriers in my chase to live out The Dream, to have the potential to get those things that would prove me equal, like I made it. But The Dream isn't really all it's cracked up to be, is it? Naturally, the more advantages one has in obtaining the tools needed for basic survival, the better. But even now, and this goes for anybody, my degrees, these pieces of paper, mean less and less in terms of comfortable earning power, as many from the so-called Generation X era can attest to. Coupled with the ever-increasing influence of corporate power over individual lives, we have to ask: was the American Dream ever a realistic possibility? We work harder for less to get basic needs, let alone wants. So, really, what are we doing all of this for? Do we get anything of real value in return for our obedience to the American Way? Can I, as a black man, move into any neighborhood in this country and be accepted as a complete human being, an assumed aspect of the American Dream? Can I assume that I'll always have the same opportunities as my white counterparts? Can we ever get to a point where *all* Americans can have the opportunity to live comfortably and not just scratch out a survivalist experience, or is that too much of a dream?

I wanted to chase that American Dream just like everybody else, but I think the problem lies in that the American Dream is mostly based on the material; i.e. money. Not that money's bad, but considering that this country chose, depended upon, and prospered with profits from slavery over moral decency, you gotta ask, is money the root of all evil? And since America has kept blacks from equal access to the chase for acquisition, we tend to incorporate the desire for material things into the desire for general equality and recognition as people.

Everybody needs a job and a decent place to cook food in. But look at some of the Founding Fathers of this country, the ones that tricked us into this whole "Dream" thing. Did some of them not live in excess: gentile white guys in mansions and on plantations with more money than they needed, owning other human beings and exploiting the poor for their revolution [I don't want to go off into history, but for more, dig up on Howard Zinn's *People's History of the United States*]? The American thing was *their* thing. Equality, freedom, the pursuit of happiness; those are just ideas that, someday, we have to take to the next level. The reality of the American Dream is to scrap and fight and collect as much as possible, usually at someone else's expense. Is this burden of "progress," – status and wealth, wealth slowly accumulating into the hands of fewer and fewer people – all we have to inherit from the Founding Fathers?

What good is it to be middle or upper class if you're miserable and can't enjoy life? Who says it's good to work ridiculous hours, bogged down with a drive for material excess, a drive inherited from men who couldn't give a shit about anybody who wasn't like them, the same men who got us locked into race and class conflict?

I can't think about this without thinkin' about my participation in the ABC program. Not that ABC told any of us we should be professionals, and that we should chase material splendor. Technically, ABC was supposed to open us to anything we wanted, but becoming a professional was one of the unspoken, inherent ideals of the program's purpose, an extenuation of that American Dream. As far as I could tell, most of us in the program were concerned about getting good grades and going to a good school so we could come out and make loot. Education and learning were side dishes. The chase for money was why I left the Bronx to go to a lily-white high school. It's why I went to Georgetown. It's why I went to grad school. It's mostly why we all do what we do, for necessity and for bullshit we don't need. We take it for granted that this is the way we're supposed to live. We're not encouraged to be individuals, to use our imagination to make things better. We're encouraged to follow the program and not to ask too many questions, despite the fact that the pursuit of happiness is ever-more elusive.

For ten years, my focus was foggy. I didn't know how to validate myself.

Degrees didn't do it. The prospect of being some bu-jee-ass, middle-class carbon copy didn't do it. I didn't want a job where I'd have to numb out for the sake of being able to say, "Look at me. I made it. I'm the shit." The dream wasn't all it was cracked up to be. I couldn't see the value of the degrees I earned, value measured in dollars and cents. I was lookin' for something else, my own thing, an ideal that seemed more normal to me than the questionable pursuits of this dream and how we identify ourselves.

The track I had been ridin' on was getting more and more narrow. What I had been striving for felt like an illusion. The ideas of what we consider black and white are illusions. Issues of race and class have us bound up in a complicated web of illusion. So fuck it. However "black" I am is gonna have to be good enough. I'm proud to be black, whatever it means, but I'm more than that. I was beginning to understand that my being – who I am – and my purpose – what I'm supposed to do with my life – could only be defined by me. Any other definition, however valid, could never speak to the truth of our individual experiences. *That* is true democracy for everyone; a way of being that still lurks in the shadows of the one dollar, one vote pseudo democracy we've come to know.

I was lookin' for something, my own thing, but unfortunately, I still had to pay bills.

While I indulged a desire to think outside the box we think of as the "American Way," I temped in some of New York's most prestigious companies, including DLJ, Union Swiss bank, and ING Bearings. Even though I knew I didn't want anything to do with life in corporate America, I always felt a pressure to join the bandwagon. It was most always economic pressure. Each time I came close to a full time gig, I was glad that it fell through. While I can't claim that any two of these places were the same, I was usually one of maybe two or three blacks in a particular office. I grew abhorrent to this kind of situation, not because of the discomfort of usually being one of the only blacks, but at the culture and mindset of the whites that I recognized from high school, college, and graduate school. I was always in situations that kept me on edge.

By this time, I had grown used to it, and I knew how to be congenial, friendly, and hardworking without giving the illusion that I gave a shit. I knew my roles in these places weren't permanent. As a temp, my invisibility was useful as opposed to frustrating. I gave people head glances to see how they saw me seeing them, just to see how they'd respond to me. There were varieties of responses, but much more ambiguity than actual acknowledgement of my person. That may not be so much a black/white thing as it is a general coldness inherent with corporate culture. But again, throw in the race issue, and it becomes so much more apparent.

One incident typifies why I think I'd eventually snap if I had to work in that kind of atmosphere for too long. Two white guys approached a secured entrance. One guy fumbled for his ID card, so instead of watchin' him go through all of that, I pulled the door open and held it for them. Not only did the bastards not say thank you, but one guy also pointed to a stack of trash and said, off-handedly, "Take care of that."

It wasn't until he turned back to me and said, "Oh, I thought you were someone else," that I realized he was originally talking to me. Wearing a dress shirt, tie, and khakis, I didn't think I looked much like a janitor. Even still, the cold, off-handed way he said it... I was wondering who *was* the poor guy that had to take that kind of demeaning shit.

It was a subtle thing, almost nothing. But those almost-nothing moments add up over time. If African-Americans didn't learn to let that kind of shit roll off our backs, white men wouldn't have the lock on serial killing. Imagine this happening thousands of times a day, everyday, all over corporate America in similar circumstances. What you have in subtleties today is what you had blatantly for hundreds of years; the unwritten statement that blacks are somehow not quite as up there as whites.

If I was ever turned off by the idea of workin' 9 to 5 for the rest of my life, which I was and still am, my year spent temping in corporate America after I got my graduate degree, solidified that idea. No amount of money seemed worth the long hours and the racial/professional politics. But I was in a funky situation. I was a non-professional master's degree holder: middle-class educated but poor. Not "inner-city," but not really middle class. Not centered, not happy.

September '96 to September '97 was the worst year of my life, burrowing from one crappy temp job to another, the money all going to credit card debt and loans from school. I was still livin' at home with no vision of a future, no goals, and my sense of worth damn near vanquished while searching for something I couldn't name.

A different type of luck bailed me out of sloth this time. It was a clue to the aimlessness I was swimming in. In the winter of 1996-97, months after receiving my graduate degree, I received an invitation to a 25th anniversary reunion of my high school's participation in the ABC program. Good ole' ABC, the benevolent program that provided me, a black child from the Bronx, an opportunity to chase that American Dream, which left me feelin' like I was in endless purgatory. When I was feelin' my lowest, I got an invite to return to the place that set me on this path.

Alan: Up Against A Lot Here

"This song (Sheryl Crow's "If It Makes You Happy") *reminds me of when I was in Atlanta, in ad school, just fucking depressed as hell. I had no car, and I couldn't go anywhere; life just sucked. There're a few songs I have on tape like that. I'm convinced that those songs were the only things that fucking kept me going, bruh.*

"I didn't know anybody. I was thrust into this situation with all these white people. On first sight, they think they know what talented people are. I definitely felt a racial barrier there. I don't know if it was self-imposed or what. It was the first time I felt that in a long time. Like, I wasn't intelligent enough to write ads. I think people expect a certain amount of intelligence that you bring to advertising. Whether that's true or not, I don't know. But when it comes to wit and intelligence, black people don't have it. I felt like they just didn't respect me.

"I was miserable. MISERABLE. I felt this blockade between my peers and myself. I'm man enough to admit that as a creative person, I like to get a certain amount of attention in general. I happen to be more conscious of that than your average Schmoe in a creative field. It's a big, pet peeve of mine, and it's something that I don't know if I'll ever get over, but sometimes, when I'm around white people and they're having a conversation, and somehow I'm not included with their eye contact, it's a problem. People speak; what is it – communication consists of 90% body language, 10% verbal language? If you're looking at one another, and not looking at me, that's telling me you don't want me in the conversation.

"That's where all that shit starts; right there. *'We have decided whether subconsciously, or consciously, that you're not included. You are different. Go somewhere else. We're not talking to you.' And the more you feel that, the more you feel like an outsider, the more you feel that 'I'm not apart of this.' The longer that goes on, the more there's a rift, and the next thing you know, they're in the club, you're not in the club, so how the fuck are you gonna break through it, you know what I'm sayin?*

"It's so sensible and so logical to me, yet people don't see it. If you were to explain that to somebody, they'd think you were crazy. '(Whining) Haaaw, they weren't looking at me in the conversation. I felt bad. I got my feelings hurt.' They'd say, 'Get the fuck outta here with that bullshit, crybaby motherfucka. GROW UP!'

"But it's very truthful. I'd be at a corporate meeting and I would ask questions or make comments at times, and they would never answer them to me, they would answer them among each other. They weren't involving me. They could give a fuck about my ass. That shit wore on me, especially at a time when I had no woman, no car, no money, no friends, and these motherfuckas were just talking among themselves.

"Especially my roommate, Rick. He was the worst. We'd be at home, hangin' out, bonding, had a lot in common, but as soon as we got around people at school, he couldn't wait to shut me out of a conversation. He was the worst. Some white people are worse at that than others. Some white people have never grown up

around black people, and they just don't understand how to talk to black people. It's just not in their modus operandi to deal with black people. He was that kind of motherfucka.

"It was depressing me. I was like, 'Well Alan, you realize that this is just a microcosm for what it's gonna be like when you get into the real world? If it's happening on this level, what about the next?'

"My experience with white people, because I've grown up around them and I'm very familiar with them, even though many of them aren't that familiar with black people, gives me an advantage; I know their game tight as hell. Once you break them down, and hang out with them enough, they can see you... 'Oh, wow, a human being! Imagine that! You're like me. You're not too much different than me!' Once they understand that, then it can be cool. But it takes a while. Once white people meet each other it's like, 'Bam! We're cool.' But when they meet other people, it takes them a long time to get past that, before they accept them.

"I had this horrible problem with my roommate. I was roomed with one of these hotshots, probably one of the premiere copywriters at our school at the time. We competed a lot. We were both sort of big shit, but everybody assumed he was the better writer. I think a lot of it had to do with the fact that he was white, but I also think it had a lot to do with the fact that people were easily baffled by his bullshit. A teacher once told me, 'Bullshit Baffles Brains.' BBB he used to always call it. So this guy was a pretty intelligent guy, very well read. He had all the natural makings for what one would assume to be a good, all-star copywriter. And he was white.

"I'm a pretty articulate guy. I'm not that well read and I'm black, so when they put us against each other, they're always going to assume that he is the better copywriter. My whole thing is that those people didn't understand what advertising is all about. Advertising is...yes; you're a writer. Yes, you need a strong command of the English language, and yes, it would certainly help that you're well read, but it doesn't have that much to do with that. It's got some kind of deeper thing going on that no one can explain. It's an innate knowledge of human nature. I would never say that in an interview, but I've been honing that craft all my life.

"I've always had that ability to empathize. That's the cornerstone of good advertising: empathy. So I don't care how erudite you are, or how many Shakespeare plays you've read, if you don't have empathy, that shit doesn't matter at all. I've seen it time and time again: people who are well read completely not knowing anything about advertising. By the same token, I don't claim to be a novelist. I couldn't go out there and write a novel. I would stumble over a short story. I don't necessarily think that I can write long prose. That's a skill in itself. All I know is how to relate to people.

"That's why I feel people don't get it, which is, unfortunately, a majority of the people in this business. They assume a lot. They look at the superficialities. 'Oh, Rick came from a good school, he's a Rhode's scholar; of course he's a good copywriter.' There's plenty of motherfuckas who are like...truck drivers, who get into this business and go on to become brilliant stars. It's a weird sort of thing because somehow, they have that innate ability to know human nature.

"I had to deal with this whole Rick thing. I used to get mad all the time. It

wasn't a matter of comparison, like, 'Rick is better than Alan,' but Rick was the star, and Alan was not. I knew the whole time...I don't know how I knew, but I knew that I was more talented than he, even though I wasn't necessarily demonstrating it at the time. I would have to suck it up a lot. I figured, 'Well, you know what, over time, people will see it. Initially, I'm always going to be at a loss.'

"During our first semester, we did these female detective ads that won awards. We were paired up, and we wrote them together, when we were really good friends. I guess in the end, I'd have to say that I probably had the most input in terms of doing the overall writing, like 65% to 35%. I wrote most of it. I remember distinct moments in our concept meetings where I had to take control of it because he just didn't know what was going on. Eventually, we got it together. That campaign was probably the most successful thing of my entire career at school. It won more awards than anything I did.

"The thing about this...it gets complicated. Rick and I wrote these lines together, and we won awards for them, but people were quick to assume that Rick was the mastermind behind that campaign, not me. I remember hearing, 'Did you see Rick's campaign on the wall,' never hearing my name. I heard that a couple of times. I remember even at the end of that quarter, when we were getting our final evaluations, our teacher had one on one meetings with us. He said a few things to Rick that suggested that he thought Rick was gonna be a real superstar in this business, and he gave me marginal feedback.

"Oh yeah, Rick wound up getting an A in that class, and I wound up with a B or a C, I don't remember. It was something below what I deserved. I think the guy just really thought that I didn't write those lines, and that it was Rick, and I just happened to be in the room when they were written.

"Further, Rick was a big kiss ass. He would always speak up in class. His objective, and I could see it very clearly in every class that I had with him, was to kiss the instructor's ass, to try and get a really good grade, which was stupid because getting a good grade in our school didn't matter. What mattered was the work. I guess this teacher was sold on Rick's bullshit in class. He just decided, in some subconscious way, that Rick was the talented one. Him being more talented, it was only logical to assume that he was the one who wrote those lines. This is one of the things that really led me to be miserable my first year. It was blatantly an act of some sort of prejudice.

"This was at the end of the first quarter. That was when I realized, 'Damn, I'm up against a lot here. This kind of shit is foul.' I don't worry about blatant forms of racism. This was very covert shit, but how would I sound complaining about the fact that Rick was getting all of the attention? If I were to make a stink about it, it would make ME look foul. I couldn't prove anything, and anybody who's really talented shouldn't have to go out of his or her way to toot their own horn. If they have to complain, then obviously they're insecure. Obviously, they're not confident. Obviously, they're not talented.

"I think this sort of shit happens a lot in college all the time. People who are in their instructor's face, who go visit them during office hours, stand a greater chance of getting a better grade than a guy whose name the teacher doesn't even know. That's life right there. But I'm sure it was exasperated by the fact that I was

black. Again, I don't know which played more of a role.

"Beyond that, I remember people in the class getting A's who just didn't do shit, and I got a marginal grade. I remember feeling very disappointed by that. I felt that my work was superior to other people's work.

"The next quarter, Rick and I got put together AGAIN. It was so random how it happened. In school, they just randomly pair you up, so we got paired up to work on another assignment. I was so mad at that. I didn't want to be on the same team with him. It was a catch-22 situation. If we fucked up, we fucked up, and that would already suck. If we did great, everybody would assume that Rick did it, so I couldn't reap the benefits in terms of jockeying and getting the notoriety that I DEFINITELY needed if I wasn't going to be in Rick's shadow the whole time.

"We came up with another brilliant campaign for Sony PlayStation, which eventually won awards. I honestly have to say that in this case, Rick had most of the input this time. I was still so bummed out that he got so much of the attention from the last campaign, off of my insight, that I didn't give a damn this time. I let it go.

"Rick was talented, don't get me wrong. He just wasn't as brilliant as everyone thought he was. He wanted to get out of school early. He didn't want to have to start showing his real ass and ruin the glory that he created for himself at school. He finished his portfolio really early. You can leave whenever you feel your portfolio is ready. By the time he started to leave, people started to see that he duded just like the rest of us. Once he was gone, there was really no one there that could steal my fame away from me. That's when I started kicking ass. Eventually, I started winning awards. People started to take notice.

"Every quarter they have a student awards show. People submit ads, and the school gives students various gold, silver, and bronze awards, and your work goes up on the wall for the next quarter. Every quarter I was there I was on the wall. None of my other classmates can claim that. I was winning awards the whole time that I was there, but people were still giving me this, 'Well, it's luck' kinda thing. For the first two or three quarters, people didn't give me my props, even though I won awards. I think that's human nature in general.

"But then I won this 'Show South' thing. The southern region has this awards show with agencies and stuff. There're three schools that participate. I wound up winning a gold and a silver in that. That was huge. That's what made people finally start to recognize me.

"From that point on, by the time I left, I was like, 'god.' It's amazing how much people respected me. I never felt that much respect from any group of people in my life. It was almost too much for me to handle. Even at graduation, the president of the school gave a little speech about me. It was totally wild."

Lie If You Have To

I got the call sometime in December of 1996 from Susan. She was my ABC host mother back in high school. Each of the ABC students had host parents. They were our families away from home. We would spend time with them on the weekends, mostly on Sundays. They'd take us to basketball or football games, cook dinner, take us shoppin', or whatever. I guess the idea was that they were learnin' somethin' from us inner city kids, and we from them. And it gave our resident director a break from us.

Susan and her husband John were decent host parents. I got along good with them and their three sons. John III was the same year as me. He'd grown up in Philly, so bein' around black kids was nothin' new to him. Still, we didn't talk or hang out too much in school. John III was a two-sport letterman, down with the Alpha clique. We didn't have much in common except for the fact that his parents volunteered for ABC.

What I liked most about Susan was that she didn't look at me as just a charity case. Even if we didn't talk about it openly, she understood the issues I had. She didn't try to impose white, upper-middle class values on me or try to change me. We did a diverse range of activities, from something like going to an African art exhibit to attending "Les Miserables."

Susan was always good about keeping in touch with Moms and me when I graduated high school. She included us on her family's Christmas card list every year, giving updates on how they were doin'. They gave me two hundred bucks when I graduated college. I wasn't just a phase in their lives.

I was still a little surprised when Susan called me that December in '96. It had been about three or four years since I actually talked to her. I rarely, if ever, called or wrote to her, partly out of laziness, partly 'cuz I felt like I didn't have shit to show, an undeserved shame I heaped on myself for having a master's degree and still no job.

I knew that her call wasn't just social. She was callin' to tell me about a 25-year anniversary reunion her and some other volunteers were putting together for Radnor ABC. When the words rolled off her tongue, I cringed. I didn't want to go back to Radnor. I hadn't been there in six years, and the thought never crossed my mind that I ever would go back. Her calling me at that time was a weird turn. I'd been having consistent dreams about being back at Radnor ever since I graduated from Fairfield, months before I knew about the reunion.

I told her I'd go, but I wasn't committed to the idea. The reunion wasn't until May '97, so I had plenty of time to think about it. But time has a way of being sneaky. April rolled around, and I got a reminder call, this time from a woman who was the main organizer of the event. It caught me off guard. I wasn't quick enough to give a last minute excuse for not going. But if I really didn't need to go, I would've gladly lied to her ass. I knew I had to go, like when you know you have to get a rectal exam when your itchy intestines are hangin' out of your ass. There was something I needed to examine.

I borrowed Moms' reliable '89 Corolla and took the two and a half-hour drive down the Jersey and Pennsylvania Turnpikes, my heart beating wildly the whole ride down. What was there to be nervous about? The fact that I didn't have a permanent job despite all of that education? Would I be some kind of let-down, some kind of failure compared to the other alumni? Or was it the fact that I really didn't want to go but felt that I had to? The truth was that I was scared to come face to face with whatever it was I didn't want to be reminded of.

I arrived at Susan's house first to meet up with her and John II before going to the reunion. We greeted each other warmly, but I had some trepidation. I stepped back within myself with the intention of examining everyone, examining how I related to everyone, even her. I hoped that she and John II couldn't see through my purpose in bein' there. It wasn't a social thing for me. It was more like a spy mission, a calling to see if I could find clues to fill in the blanks on the question mark forming boldly in my mind. Susan and I ended up talking about it after I got over the jitters of not having seen them in a while. I told her that I didn't know exactly why I came, but that it wasn't entirely social. She understood, replying, with an empathetic tone, "Maybe there's something you need to settle."

I didn't think about this until later, but when we sat down to talk, she and John sat together on a couch clear across the room from the chair I was sitting in. I don't know if the positioning simply worked out that way, but it was indicative of the distance I was feelin'. We exchanged the usual pleasantries, catching up. But that distance between us was weird. It almost felt like I was in an interview more than with friends. In my mind, I took a few more steps backward.

We had some time to kill before the reunion reception, and she had made plans to visit a friend of hers who was holding a Kentucky Derby party in one of the neighboring towns. A fucking Kentucky Derby party. Can you believe that shit? Susan didn't really want to go either, but she was sorta obligated. She said she'd understand if I didn't want to go, and that I could wait at the house until they got back. Then we'd go to the reunion. I didn't want to be by myself, though, especially in their house. It was huge. And I was feelin' just about as small inside of myself as I felt in that house. I wasn't lookin' forward to the reunion, and any company I had, no matter what or where, made me feel better. I reluctantly tagged along to the derby party.

Before we left, there was something we decided to settle. Obviously, there'd be questions when those upper-class lilies saw my skinny black ass with Susan and John. We decided that we'd tell them I was one of Susan's former students rather than go into the whole ABC story. Thing is, Susan taught Special Ed. For a brief, brief nano-second, I was gonna object. But I can't tell you how many times people would ask me, "Where'd you go to high school?" I'd tell them outside of Philadelphia. Then they'd ask, "But aren't you from New York?" Then I'd have to go into this whole schpeel, "Well, I was part of this program called ABC. ABC is a non-profit organization that gives inner-city kids…" Without knowin' every single ABC alumni there is to know, I can go out on a limb and say that every single one of us, at some point, was sick of explaining it all.

When I told people the story, I usually got, 'Oh, how nice…' like I was a rehabilitated retard. How would you feel tellin' somebody you were part of a program called ABC? I know it isn't Special Ed, but doesn't it sound like it? It took me years to boil it down to, "It's kinda like boarding school."

Susan was right. I didn't feel like gettin' into it, even if I had to pass as a Special Ed alum. As long as we knew what was up, it didn't matter. That was one of the things I liked about us. We were often on the same wavelength.

After about forty-five minutes of being dunked in upper-class hell, we made our way to the reunion. We pulled up to the house where the reception was being held. I took a deep breath and started walking up the driveway. The first person we ran into was a man I remembered as Mr. McKenna, a Special Ed teacher at Radnor. I never knew his first name, but the ABC students always thought he was cool. I'm not sure how he was officially associated with the program. In my senior year, he put me in the student versus faculty basketball game, which really amounted to a shit-grinning popularity contest. One of the cool kids declined, and McKenna asked me if I wanted to play. At least I got a chance to feel cool for a night. I even scored a basket. I liked him for that.

We greeted each other sincerely, the same as we did back when I was in school. We did the usual, 'Hi, how's it going' routine. But I didn't mind going through the routine with him. When I asked him how he was doing, he sarcastically slipped in the fact that he was unsure of his future job security at the school. It was bothering him enough to mention it to me, a person he hadn't seen in eight years. I felt bad because within those few minutes, I had confirmed that he wasn't one of the fake ones. One down, dozens to go.

We continued up the driveway to a large house hidden behind tall trees. The owners were obviously wealthy and happy to host a reunion for us special ABC kids. My radar was on full alert. I decided to cling immediately to the first person I knew I'd be comfortable with. It turned out to be a small group of fellow alumni who lived with me when I was a student. I wasn't surprised to see them. We had a lot of fun in the house back then.

There was one person in particular I was glad to see: Rik, a Mexican-American from New York, who graduated a year after me. We used to bug out like madmen. We got in trouble all the time in our English class for goofin' off and crackin' jokes, so much so that the teacher had to set us across the room from each other. How could we take *Wuthering Heights* seriously? Rik's one of those guys who's forever ready to crack a joke, have a snappy comeback, or otherwise make you look bad for a good laugh, but always in good nature. Out of all the other people there, he was the one I was closest to back in the day. I decided that he'd be the safest bet to hang around that night.

There were about seven more of my old housemates there with whom I had varying degrees of friendship. Our resident director Jesse was there, too. I thank God to this day that he was as cool as he was. He went through the whole routine of being an ABC student, so he knew how to handle us. With one exception, there were no major problems in the house while he was the RD, at least while I was there.

Most of the students I lived with got along with each other back in the day, and we were all glad to see each other, but I wasn't feelin' much of a connection with any of them. Years of growth and separation made me feel like we were strangers. After the first deluge of hugs and conversation, the delight of the first encounter was over, and the reception became another drab social event where you're struggling to find words to keep conversation goin'. The atmosphere was stiff and rigid. It could've just been me in my passive-observer mode. Most of the faces in the house were older and white. I scanned the faces, looking to see if I could establish eye contact, to possibly begin a conversation with someone I didn't know, or anyone who was willing. No takers. Then something strange occurred to me. Outside of the group of students I knew, there were only two other alumni in the place: one who graduated in the early eighties before I did, and one who graduated in the early nineties after me, and then Jesse. That made a total of around 11 alumni. Eleven; most of whom lived in the house when I was there. I tried to think of the reasons why there was such low attendance. Since it was supposed to be a 25-year anniversary, I thought that perhaps the organizers had simply lost contact with the earliest alumni. Maybe people had other plans for the weekend. Maybe others just didn't know about it. But still; only eleven alumni? What about the most recent grads who should have been reachable? Twenty-five years worth of alumni and only one house-full show up?

I walked around for a little while, gettin' drinks to numb the dullness, seein' if my senses were playing with me. There were only a few other blacks there besides the alumni, including an older black couple who were ABC board members at one time or another. I bumped into some other board members that I knew from my tenure, who were still active in the program. It was weird observing them as an adult. When I was a student, I looked at the ABC board members and volunteers as authority figures, to a certain degree, and with a certain amount of deference. But it was different at the reunion. Our roles with each other had changed. I felt like an equal adult human being, not the charity case minority student. This role change made things a little uncomfortable; it was hard for us to move beyond the roles we were accustomed to, not much different than black and white society at large. I'd even go so far to say that a lot of people at the reunion: the board members, ex-volunteers and maybe some of the alumni really didn't want to be there as much as I didn't.

There was very little sincerity in conversations with the older folks, whizzing through auto-responses and drab formalities. There was a total lack of desire for us to really know each other. Not once was I asked anything having to do with my personal life, which I was thankful for, seeing that I didn't have one. Most questions tended to be centered on our professional lives. But they seemed like more than just casual questions. There were expectations behind them.

'Heeeey, Roooon, how are you? Good, good. And what are yooouu doing?'

'Oh, makin' $8.50 an hour temping at a job that a tenth grader could do. Theses weenies are delish', huh?'

You don't know how badly I wanted to say that. I told everybody I was permanently working for the company I was actually temping for at the time. In truth, however, I was one of, if not *the* only alumnus at the reception who *wasn't* employed full time.

I had a brief conversation with a black man, the husband of the resident director at the time, a black woman. By the way he looked and spoke, I figured he was just an average Joe and had nothing to do with the program except that his wife was the RD. I felt comfortable rappin' with him. We talked about our interests in music and the arts. Then, in so many words, we talked about how we thought the whole ABC thing was questionable at best. I told him that despite my academic success, I had doubts about the worth of it all. When his wife joined the conversation, he said to her, "See honey, he's not happy," like that was an on-going thing between them.

"Well, at least it's not just me," I thought. But I back-tracked a little when I started talking with her, explaining that it wasn't exactly the case that I wasn't happy, but that I was unsure about whether or not it was worth the downside of participating in ABC. After I tip-toed around the issue, her husband's face turned away in disgust. I felt bad about blowin' my man's point because the fact remained that I wasn't happy, but I didn't want anybody there to know that. I was spyin' on the whole scene, to find clues into my unhappiness and uncertainty, and I didn't want my cover blown. Funny thing is that I felt like *we* were being examined too.

The first time I really became annoyed was when I talked to a man who was the head of the Radnor ABC program when I was there, a man who's last name was Webb. We thought of him as a nice guy. Every now and then he gave us tickets to Phillies, Sixers, and Eagles games, and he was instrumental in getting our broken-down house refurbished, of course after I graduated. For that reason alone, I wanted to acknowledge him, even though I didn't know him well. I wasn't even sure that he'd remember me. When I expressed this concern to Rik, he assured me that Webb would remember. Rik pulled me over and said, "Hey, Mr. Webb [funny how we still thought of him as "Mr."], you remember Ron, right?"

There was an ever-so-slight pause, but the smile on Webb's face never cracked. You could see him thinkin', "Ron...Ron...Ron...?" behind blank eyes. This was in brief, brief nano-seconds, but I could tell. Finally, he said, as if he were continuing a thought, "Yeah, I was just talking to Ron about how we were hoping that the program would have a ripple effect, with you guys going back to your communities to make a difference."

What? Maybe that was my evil twin, or actually another alumnus named *Rob*, who doesn't look anything like me, by the way. I wonder how Rob responded to this "ripple effect" shit that sounded too much like Reagan's "trickle-down" shit. Did this guy see me as a person or as an experiment to an idea?

I didn't speak to any other board members for the rest of the reception. I was content to crack jokes with Rik.

After the reception, we went to the ABC house for dinner. I hadn't seen the new renovations, and when I saw them I was amazed and jealous. When I lived there, it was old with ugly, puke-beige paint chippin' off the walls, and the staircase was lopsided and creaky. The house was on its last leg. The improvements were astounding and elicited many 'You should be glad...' comments from the alumni to the current students.

One of the tutors and the students hooked up a slammin' meal of ribs, ham, baked chicken: the works. In situations like that, I try to be on my best behavior when it comes to pilin' too much food on my plate, for courtesy sake. I try to watch my table manners and all that good stuff. So I was pissed when one board member greedily snatched ribs and devoured them veraciously, like a big, bearded beaver chewing hungrily and half-paying attention to a conversation someone was trying to hold with him.

In the middle of the feast, another board member, a funny-lookin' black dude with big, thick glasses, a beard, receding hairline, and an even funnier name [which I won't disclose out of courtesy] gave a little speech. It was the usual schpeel about how good it was to see the alumni, and how he wanted us to go around the table and say our names, where we were from, what our experiences were like being in the program, where we went to school, what jobs we had, any advice for the kids in the program... Thankfully, Jesse spoke up about how absurd it would be for us to go through all of that during dinner, so we gave the abbreviated version of our lives.

As we went around the table, some very prestigious names were thrown around and about. Brown University. Vasser College. University of Pennsylvania. 'I work for Citicorp.' 'I work for JP Morgan.' 'I'm an account person for Kraft.' 'Time Warner.' One alum nervously threw in the fact that she was flying to London the following week on business, which initiated even more 'oohs' and 'ahs,' head-nodding approval, and satisfaction on everyone's faces.

Well, at least these guys turned out okay, I thought.

Even though I didn't have a job with a top company, I could still represent with my academic resume, but I was lifeless and told my story with low vigor, like I wanted everybody to know that it wasn't such a big deal. Where did this shit get me? Am I the only one raising questions, like some deep shit-type questions? I wanted to say that I thought it was all bullshit, and that the game was rigged, but hey, why should I have been the pooper?

After dinner, a few of the alumni went to the carriage house behind the main house, where the male students lived. The place had that sweaty feet, dormitory feel to it, and seemed like a somewhat cramped living space for four boys to live in. I wanted to see how they were dealing with their situation. They seemed glad to be away from home, as I was, but what surprised me was that they seemed to like going to school more than they liked being in the ABC house. For me, it was the opposite. We had some good times screwin' around in the house. But they felt that the rules they had to obey were too strict, like limited phone time, not being able to leave the house without another person accompanying them, and other requirements like confirmation of where they were going, who they were with, and a phone call from the other party.

At first, I didn't believe them. I thought they were exaggerating. But they all confirmed, and I thought, *My God, what happened? Not bein' able to leave the house by yourself?* What the hell could possibly happen in a town like Radnor? I understand the accountability issues, but it seemed like a crackdown compared to when I was there. I didn't like hearing these things. A resentment that was already there was brewing further to the surface. Even though I had freedom when I was living there, I didn't like the idea that the board members could restrict these kids' freedom. It was just one more reason to seethe.

Apparently, things got shaky the year after I graduated. A white couple, a high school science teacher and his wife, became resident directors after Jesse and his family left. When I was a senior, Susan had asked me what I thought about having a white couple from the town as the RDs. I told her that I didn't think it would be a good idea. The students needed somebody that could relate to them like Jesse did with us. But it didn't turn out that way, as relayed to me by Rik after the reunion.

Rik told me, *"I was thinking about Mr. Elliot, the science teacher. He's a nice guy and all of that. I'd see him around school, and I'd think, 'What a nice guy.' I mean, the guy was like Mr. Rogers. But it was really his wife that ran the house. She's the one that wore the pants. She's the one that enforced the rules. And these rules were ridiculous. For example, it would be like ten o'clock at night, after study hall, and we'd be up in the room talkin' bullshit, watching Arsenio Hall, talkin' every night about anything and everything. She would come into the room and be like, 'You guys are not supposed to talk.' And we'd be like, 'What?'*

"They gave us a list of rules. There was always a handbook, but it was obvious shit, like no smoking pot in your room. And I'm sure there was some legal shit. The program would get busted for shit like that. That's what the fucking rulebook was for. But they were harping on every little rule. Not being allowed to watch TV at night? So she'd be like, 'No television and you guys gotta stop talking,' but she'd leave the room, and we'd be like, 'Whatever.' We'd turn the TV off and just keep talking.

"One time Mr. Elliot called us into his office saying that he needed to talk to us. He said, 'Listen, my wife has told me that she warned you guys about the TV thing and about talking late at night, and that you guys got to stop at 10:30.' You had to see our faces. I mean, we're city kids, and this guy is like Mr. Rogers. He'd say it in such a nerdy way; we didn't know whether to laugh or what. We were like, 'Is he serious?' We thought it was a joke. And he was like, 'We can't have that.'

"And then he threatened us by saying, 'Well, if you continue, we'll take some of your privileges, like TV.' Stuff like that. They'd unplug or take it away or something like that. You know how, like, when you're little and you bring a little GI Joe figure to school, and you act up and the teacher takes it away until the end of the day? It was like that.

"There was this one guy on the ABC board. He was black. I think his name was Duane. He tried to help us out. But it got to a point where we felt like he was just talking shit. It was all talk. We were tellin' him that they didn't understand us; we come from two different words. I didn't grow up watching Mr. Rogers. Now all of a sudden I have to live with him?

"It was difficult, and they really didn't understand. Maybe if we were watching 'Letterman' or something, it'd be different. I don't know. Certain things are understandable, but they have to understand that we come from the inner cities. For example, the way we talk. I curse a lot. I have the dirtiest fuckin' mouth. I do. I mean, fuck, shit; there're like adjectives to me. It's incredible. I understand, "Don't curse," or whatever, but you have to understand, you are not our parents.

"Remember when we used to play basketball? It didn't matter if the ground was covered in snow. We'd be out there shoveling that shit, playing with thick-ass gloves on. If it rained, we'd have gauchos on. One more game turned into five.

And if it got too late, Jesse would call us in. But it got to a point where we couldn't even play during certain hours of the weekend because Mr. Elliot said that we were disturbing the neighbors; like in the daytime, or in the morning, we couldn't play. We loved to play. I mean, what else was there to do?

"I would have never noticed until Rob said something, like, they're trying to bring their "white" ideas. I mean, I'm Hispanic and I kinda felt, like, in the middle, but I'm still a minority. I could relate to everybody because I had white friends growing up. But when he said that, I was like, 'Yeah, you're right.'

"The only thing that kept me, Rob, and Anthony from getting kicked out was that we stuck together. There were times when I wasn't sure Anthony was 100% right, but I supported him. And Rob especially... The one thing about Rob, he was my roommate, the pain in the ass. Sometimes I hated him. We got into fights all the time but because of everything that was happening, I grew to love the guy. I really appreciated him. I feel like he was my brother through hard times.

"It got to a point where Anthony and I were fighting with [the board] all the time. We were the ones most vocal about the things that we thought were wrong. And we were the ones who got in trouble the most. I even called my mother one night, crying, because I was so upset about the situation. But the good thing is we survived it all, we achieved our goal. The fucking Elliots are gone.

"I'm not knocking the program. I would say good things about the program anyway. It's not a perfect world. But shit like that was happening my last year there. I felt like people were trying to cover shit up. Rich got kicked out. The other kid dropped out, and then Sarnetta and Melissa got kicked out. I think they started getting nervous. But I'd still say good things about the program."

Jesse lived a few miles from the ABC house with his family. After dinner, the alumni went to his crib to have our own little reunion. I was personally relieved to be able to let down my guard a bit. The first part of the spy mission was over. Most of those lilies weren't people that I wanted to know or be like. Next, I was lookin' to see if any of the other alumni had anything close to the thoughts I was havin'. They all fell into the "professional" category and seemed to be doin' okay.

When I rode over to Jesse's house with this one alumni, I asked him how he was doin' with a personal inflection in my tone. He said, "Oh, I'm happy. I'm very happy," with no noticeable smile on his face. I wasn't sure if he was tryin' to convince himself or me. Another young fella, straight outta school, was already hatin' the nine to five grind but had huge loans to pay off. Other than that, I really couldn't get into anyone's mind to affirm any of the thoughts I had about the roads we traveled after participating in ABC. It might've just been me, but I sensed something underneath the nostalgia and the awkward silences, but I couldn't get at it, and I didn't have the courage to just come out and ask, "Is anyone else here feelin' less than whole?"

Ah, fuck it; it must've just been me. Aimless, clueless, not happy with the opportunities I had, not maximizing them to my benefit. Maybe I was still just The Grouch, pouting at God knows what, like a bratty adolescent.

But still, by the end of brunch on Sunday afternoon, I was ready to jet. I couldn't stand bein' there. The mission was over. I took inventory of the memorable occurrences: the stiff formalities of the reception, the lack of feeling from those who were volunteering for the program, the insincerity, the feeling of having been a lab rat, and the unspoken tension bottled up like a Jack in the Box.

The material benefits of the program are obvious, at least for those who maximize their opportunities. But there's more to it than that. I had a feelin' that even though most of the other alumni there had what would be considered good jobs, they got caught up in that whole game-of-life, role-playing thing, the whole idea that there's not more to life than school-job-retire-die. I didn't feel bad about not being as "successful" as the other alumni if it meant slowin' down the race to be a corporate drone, for fucking up and living life the way I wanted to for a while.

But I can't shit on anyone's goals just because I didn't have any. At the same time, I wondered if any of the alumni there were living their lives the way they wanted to, the way their hearts wanted them to. I wondered if they got caught up in the idea that this was the way they were supposed to live, whether it was from the ideals of the program, or of that thing we call the American Dream.

I couldn't have been the only alumnus thinking this. What about all the others that weren't there? Whatever their reasons for not coming, the fact that so few alumni showed up is telling of how much the program was missed. I certainly hadn't missed it and couldn't wait to leave again.

Before I left, two things happened that gave me more to think about. First, they took a picture of the alumni who attended the reunion. Public relations shit. Afterwards, one of the ladies was getting our names to match the faces in the picture. As we read her the names that matched the faces, she repeated them. At one point, she got two of us backwards. When someone pointed that out to her, she said, "Oh, it doesn't matter," waved it off, and continued.

"What the fuck do you mean, 'It doesn't matter,'" I thought. *"Bitch, we have names AND faces."*

I almost left on that note, but a few of the fellas started shootin' hoops behind the carriage house. I went out back with them. The main organizer of the event, the same woman who called me in April, came out to tell us that the brunch was being videotaped, and that it would be a good idea if the alumni got on camera saying good things about the program.

Silence.

There were three or four of us shootin' hoops. Rik had already left by then. No one else responded. We just kept on shootin', grabbin' rebounds, passin' the ball. I don't know if the fellas were thinkin' the same thing I was thinkin', but I had no intention of gettin' on camera sayin' anything. At best I'd be exaggerating on cue from them. I really didn't know what to say, good or bad. I wasn't gonna just be a parrot for the program.

After a few moments of silence, the woman, half-jokingly, said, "Lie if you have to. We have to keep the program going." She said it in an 'Oops, did I say that' kinda way.

Again, silence. No one said a word. I didn't acknowledge her. I took a few more shots, went back up to the main house, and said my good-byes and pleasant tidings. I tried to muster up some warmth in my goodbye to Susan, but it was hard.

All I could hear was "Lie if you have to." She told me she wished I would come down more often to visit. I told her I would, even though I was thinking I'd probably never see any of those people again, besides maybe Rik.

Cruisin' up the Pennsylvania Turnpike, I was satisfied with the mission. The doubts I had for so long, that irky feeling that crept inside my head was validated. There's more to this life's game than doing what's expected of you by those with questionable motives. All motives became questionable at that point, including my own. That woman's words heralded the beginning of an affirmation of the "I." What am I really all about, above these games, above payin' bills, eking out an existence of just gettin' by, rushing toward corporate acceptance, imitating what's supposed to be instead of being?

That woman's thoughtlessness, however off-handed, paralyzed my soul. The uneasiness with which I seemed to live the previous ten years was summed up in five words: Lie if you have to.

Alan: Damn, I'm Back in High School

"I interned for an ad agency for a year at Leo Burnett, here in Chicago. By the end of that year, there was a lot of stuff I had to go through. My boss was a real jerk. We were butting heads all the time. I finally didn't have to work for him any more for the last four months I was there. I got a chance to really get into my groove. I was totally on top of my world, feeling good, really kicking ass at work. And then before I knew it, the internship was over. I was devastated. I thought natural progression was just to move into the creative department. That never happened, so I had to go back into school.

"That confidence that I enjoyed in Chicago, it went down in grad school. It was a horrible time. I hated waiting tables to support myself. I also wasn't getting into school, with all the shit I had to go through. There was no outlet for me to have any form of enjoyment. My confidence level sunk to an all-time low. It rose up again as I was ready to leave Atlanta. I was kicking ass, doing really well, on cloud nine.

"But then again, at this new job I'm in another slump. I'm the low man on the totem pole, so I'm fighting and clawing. It's the same ole' shit: peaks and valleys. I'm waiting until I can get to the point again where I can be confident and have it stay that way for a while rather than always be like, 'Damn, enjoy it while you can, because in a couple of months, it'll be right back down to the ground again.'

"I had a lot of options coming out of ad school. I could be making lots of money. I got flown around the country and all that shit. But I decided to be paid less money and work at a less glamorous agency. I basically took a risk because I figured these people were kinda grass roots guys. [I thought] they were gonna be hungrier than a bigger, more established agency. I wanted to go with the hungrier guys because they're going to be going after the great work.

"I don't think it's necessarily paying off the way I thought it would. So what do I need to do? Rather than bellyache, I need to get the fuck out. The longer I sit around in this agency, the less opportunity I'll have to get great work sold. After a while, they'll break you. They do it subconsciously. If you know you have to do this sort of work in order for it to be sold, you'll continue to do it, and you'll forget how to do the really great work.

"I feel myself getting pigeon-holed. Lately, I've been feeling like...again, I don't know if my agency really knows what great work is. That's an issue with me. That is the most important thing to me, beyond politics and all that shit. If, for instance, they knew what great work was and I was still butting heads with bullshit politics, I would be like, 'Fuck it. At least I'm learning from these motherfuckas. Hell, they can diss me all they want, as long as I'm learning some shit.' I can eventually take what I learned and just go on elsewhere, but if I don't feel like I'm learning anything, then I'm getting screwed TWICE; I'm putting up with office politics that I don't care for, AND these motherfuckas are hacks. A hack is someone with no talent. It's a term we use in advertising.

"I think a lot of the problems that I'm having at work stem from this high school thing. I was made to feel a certain way whenever I was in a room with white

people. Not specifically white women, but white men. For some reason, they always make me feel like I should be on edge or something. And I don't necessarily think it's a racial thing. That's what's so hard to decipher. It could have just been a high school thing. I just know that a lot of the white people... not a lot of white people, but the popular group of guys [in my high school] were really witty, fast-talking, clever, sort of funny guys. There were a lot of precocious kids that went to my high school. In many ways, it was intimidating being around folks like that. I always felt a need to be clever and quick. They were the popular guys. I don't know. That could just be a typical high school situation. I can't exclude the fact that I was black in a predominantly Jewish school. That had some sort of role in it. I can't really figure out how much of a role it played.

"So now, I feel a lot of that at work. I always seem to get into this mode where I can feel it happening. I consider myself to be very quick-witted and funny. That's all an outgrowth of one's self esteem and confidence level. When someone feels more confident and their self-esteem is higher, they're prone to be quicker, or to be funny, or to be relaxed. On the other hand, if you're nervous or unsure, the quick wit isn't there. That's what I feel a lot of times when I'm at work. I can't really be me. I mean, I can be quick-witted and funny when I need to be, or when I want to be. But when I'm not feeling comfortable, I wind up clamming up. I don't know. There's just some kind of weird energy there. I've never been able to explain it. I know I get into that mode when I'm around my high school friends, which has been happening more since I been in Chicago. Whenever I come into contact with them, my first impulse is to clam up just as I did when I was in high school. Not my close friends, but acquaintances, people who were part of the core, popular group who were not my good friends when we were in school. It sort of reminds me of the people I work with now.

"When I was a kid, I never got into typical male things to do, like sports. I was just never into that. I guess a more artistic side of me already started to come out. I've never felt like sitting around, doing prototypical male things. I think that sort of added to the fact of why I was marginalized in high school, on top of all the issues of race. You couldn't go to a school like mine and survive in the core, popular crew, and I'm thinking of the few blacks that did it. In terms of me, I guess I always focus on the difference. It's always there in my head. 'I'm different than these folks.' Because of that, it's like a self-fulfilling prophecy in many ways – I'm so focused on the difference that sometimes I clam up.

"I see a hierarchy in my office just as I did when I was in high school. Right now, I'm definitely in the marginalized group, but again, it could just be due to the fact that I'm new. That's why I'm on the bottom of the totem pole. But I have this FEAR...and this is what scares me, and this is why I think about leaving all the time... that I'm ALWAYS going to be considered an outsider, hence, at the bottom of the totem pole.

"See, in advertising, television spots are where it's at. You don't really get promoted or excel until you have a kick ass TV campaign. Competition is fierce. And if there are people who have been there for ten years versus people who have been there for two years, they're not gonna let some guy come along and have all the glory. That's just human nature.

"But secondly, it's like, 'Okay, what if we did give you this commercial? That means we gotta fly out to California with your ass for three weeks in a hotel and spend eight hours a day with your ass. Frankly, I don't know if I like you enough to spend eight hours a day with you. You're kinda quiet. You sit around the office. No one seems to know what you're about. What the hell do I want to be around you for?'

"It goes back to that issue of 'coolness,' like in high school. 'Shit, I like Barry. That's my man, so of course I want him to get the television spot. We're gonna go on the shoot and kick it. But Alan, fuck, that'd be a nightmare.' That's how it happens. Then it gets into an issue of popularity versus talent. So it's like, 'Damn, that popularity thing again. I'm back in high school.'

"They always told us in advertising school that every agency has a distinct culture. It may just very well be that you don't mesh with that culture. That's not anything personal. You just have to find the right culture. My bigger fear is, well fuck, is EVERY agency like this, and I'm just fooling myself with this whole culture nonsense, or is it an issue of me just not fitting into the profession? Is this problem going to repeat itself no matter what agency I go to?

"I'm good enough to always be employed somewhere, but rising up the ranks is going to be hard for me. Until I can find a way to break out of my shell – I know I'm capable – it's just... some wall. I know these things are happening on a rational level, but emotionally, the irrational level wins all the time. At the same time, I always seem to have these tough problems. I told you before, during my first year of ad school, I hated it. Now with this job, I feel like, again, a premonition of things to come. This is what it's going to be like with all these white folks.

"I am very fortunate, and that's what I always have to tell myself because hell, I went to private schools all my life. In a sense, I have a far greater ability to understand and assimilate myself with my co-workers than an over-achieving person in public school who got good grades does. There were plenty of people in college like that, that got really good grades in high school, but only hung out with black people. They get to college and get good grades, but still only hang out with black people.

"Then what happens, when they eventually graduate after years and years of just inculcating themselves with black people, for whatever reasons, whether by choice or by environment; they get to corporate America where they may be one of two black people in the office, and they're fucking devastated. Not that that's a good thing or a bad thing, because I'm not saying they should've been hanging around white people all their lives. I'm just saying corporate America is FUCKED UP. More often than not, we're not prepared for it.

"The reasons why we're shut out and the glass ceiling is above us all aren't necessarily purely racist. That's part of it, but it's more complicated than that. I think that's what people should realize. There're cultural differences as well, and cultural differences aren't necessarily racism. How do you call somebody a racist because they're culturally different than you? For whatever reasons, we've been pushed into our roles socially and culturally. It's nobody's fault, and it's everybody's fault. It's a weird thing.

"Yes, you could argue that corporations need to take a responsibility to open *themselves to be receptive to other cultures. Managers need to make an effort to learn about varied cultures so they can manage them and incorporate diverse individuals into their groups. But then again, that's bullshit. How do you legislate that? You can't do it. It'll never happen.*

"I think anger, a lot of times, is false reaction. People are angry at The System, angry with corporate America. The anger's misplaced. It's like I said earlier, no one's to blame and everyone's to blame. It's one of those things I don't have an answer to, and I don't think I ever will. I don't know how to improve the situation. All I know how do to is try to adapt to it as best as I can. I think everybody needs to do that because I don't think that there's a universal solution."

The God-Given Path

About a month after the ABC reunion, I was scheduled to give a speech at my church in the South Bronx. Moms "suggested" that I should do it, given the fact that the church supported me financially (and spiritually, I suppose) through all the years of my schooling. I nodded at the idea of giving a speech, and at some point, it turned into a promise. I put it off after graduating Georgetown. My excuse was that I hadn't quite done anything with myself at that point. I didn't have a job, and I didn't know what I wanted to do, so what would I say? After earning my graduate degree, I couldn't stall anymore, even though I still didn't have a job and still didn't know what I wanted to do.

I resented the idea of giving a speech. I resented the fact that nobody would understand why I had resentment. What the fuck was I supposed to say? That I felt truly blessed to have an education? Was I supposed to expound to the youth of the church the virtues of going to school? Was I supposed to be some kind of role model?

"Lie if you have to. We have to keep the program going," I remembered.

That shit pissed me off. To her, it was probably just a harmless joke. Even if she meant it as such, did she take one second to think about it? What program? Whose program? Should we have lied, if we had to, to keep "the program" going for us poor, underprivileged minorities, or to continue to salve her liberal guilt, to reassure herself that she's doin' her part, regardless of how we really felt about the program? Maybe she even suspected something was amiss, judging by our silent response to her request and the relatively low turnout of alumni at the reunion.

If we did have something good to say about our experiences, wouldn't it have been more beneficial for young applicants of the program to hear the truth, at least as we saw it? Keeping the program going, for reasons she may or may not have really thought about, wasn't a good enough reason for me to lure people into it, especially when I had misgivings about its intent and purpose.

Again, the program does what it's supposed to do: it gives minorities a better chance in education and, presumably, the workforce. The politically incorrect way of putting it is that the program teaches minorities how to deal with being around white people, a social currency worth more than paper degrees. Ultimately, the program was only a symbol of a larger picture that bothered me. It was the tokenism of the program, and the fact that it was shaped and created by upper class, New England lilies who thought a "minority" like me needed to be under the care and tutelage of other lilies in order to "be somebody." I hated that the best America could do was give *some* of us a chance, separating us from those left behind by circumstance. The question is; a chance at what?

I was supposed to be happy with the chances I got, keep quiet about it like a good boy, then become some kind of recruiter used as a tool to "keep the program going." I wasn't sure of whom the real beneficiaries of "The Program" were: us underprivileged minorities who had greater access to working our way to privilege? The program of liberal upper class on a perpetually patronizing guilt trip, who didn't realize how they still keep blacks below them despite their patronage? Or is there a higher Program at work, one that keeps some of us in check with our new-found "privilege" by forcing us to fight toward assimilation into a system that grudgingly accepts us, if at all, while nothing substantial ever changes for the majority of black America?

Getting an education certainly didn't hurt me, but it was misguided. I put my time and energy into an empty chase for the Jag, an office, the comfort and security of status, the insatiable ho, with the words "Lie if you have to" as the punch line. The idea that you go to school, get your dream job, and live a comfortable life was a formless fantasy of success. I felt the furthest thing from successful. I felt like I had been bamboozled. I felt like I wasted my time and energy, distracted from myself and my real life. I spent the previous ten years chasin' a cloudy dream, and it took me ten years to figure out that it wasn't *mine*. I was fulfilling other people's hopes: the hope of my parents, the hope of black America, the ABC program's hopes, the hopes of well-meaning people who want to do what they can to ease the burdens of permanent racism, and so on. A great education can never hurt a soul, but if you're doin' it for reasons that aren't your own, what's the use?

I needed to de-program myself. I needed to start over, put everything behind me, and figure out what it was I really wanted to do with my life, regardless of whether or not I could use degrees as badges. I wanted to find success on my own terms, for reasons that were my own

But I couldn't quite do that yet. I had some lashing out to do first.

The prospect of me giving that speech at church was a big thing for Moms. Not only would it have been a time to swim in pride at the accomplishments of her baby, but it was also, to her, an affirmation of the grace of God. I went above and beyond what she and Pops had hoped for, through economic crises, through separation, and his death. Only God could've gotten us through all that.

Church was always a big part of our family, even though Pops never went. But I didn't mind goin' to church when I was young. There were always people my age to hang out with. The older folks adored me. We had blacks, whites, and Hispanics in our congregation, a reinforcement of the diversity I'd always grown up with. The church itself was a picture in grandiosity. Built in the late 1800's, it was originally meant to cater to an upper-crust society of the south Bronx, in some distant time I couldn't imagine. The sanctuary was adorned with stained-glassed windows all around, colorful mosaic puzzles of blue and red depicting various scenes from biblical folklore: Mary Magdalene kissing Jesus' foot, an angel guiding Mary and Joseph to a small barn. I admired the art and beauty; before I realized that people in the Middle East couldn't have all been lily white.

Three huge rows of finished wooden pews lay spread over the ground floor of the sanctuary, with more pews in the balcony. Not that cheap, sickly beige wood you see in these storefront churches, but that old-time, worn-looking, brown wood, worn-looking but still retaining its luster. The organ boomed but struck your ears pleasantly. The chimes from the organ stood like giant, sharp, brass pencils above and behind the pulpit. I used to imagine that Jesus was behind those chimes, bleeding in agony on a cross. I imagined waiting until the day those pencils fell and revealed his glory to the congregation.

We had three choirs: the senior choir, in black robes, sang traditional hymns the way they sing in Saint Johns Cathedral on Christmas day. Then there was the old fashioned, get down, good time gospel choir, with golden robes swaying and bouncing over the exaggerated movement from the robust bodies underneath. Finally, there was the youth choir in sky-blue robes. Some choir members did double duty, singing in the gospel choir while still wearing their black robes. I sung in the youth choir for a while, hating the fact that I was the only male soprano. You knew it was a special day when all three choirs were singing. It meant that we could act like grown-ups and drink the Welch's grape juice and eat tasteless bread, reenacting Jesus' last evening on earth.

Church was church. I fidgeted through sermons, making excuses to go to the bathroom downstairs just to break the boredom. I took the red and white peppermints from Aunt Susie, mindlessly listening to the sermons of Tom Bentz or Reverend Phillips. The thing to look for was the song at the end, when all choirs would exit their designated pews and head toward the back of the sanctuary. That was the moment I waited for all morning 'cuz that was when I knew church was over. After Moms hugged and kissed *everybody*, after they pinched my cheeks and coddled over me, I could go home, take off those tight, itchy church socks and spend the rest of the day playin' with my toys.

It rarely occurred to me that I was supposed to be getting something out of it all. When you're a kid, you don't question these things too much. At least I didn't, except for this one time I asked Reverend Phillips how Moses parted the Red Sea. Not because I wanted to know what Moses did to win God's favor. I wanted to know, logically, how a man waves a stick over a large body of water and it opens for him. He gave me a logical answer; in that era sea levels may have been relatively low during certain times of the year. One could've possibly walked through shallow waters in certain areas. The term "Parting the sea" was more poetry than fact, he said. I thought, "Oh, so in other words, don't take these things too literally."

I went through the ceremonies and rituals because I was supposed to, not because I believed any of it. I just knew I had to do it because everybody else was doin' it, and mainly, because Moms said so. I had to go to confirmation class. I had to pray. There were certain times I had to sing out of the red hymnal instead of the blue one. I had to go to Sunday school, where the teacher, Mrs. Phillips, sometimes belched and farted with a blank look on her face, like it wasn't totally disgusting. I was too confused to laugh or be disgusted.

God was impersonal and on the bottom of the list of things to worry about Monday through Saturday.

As I spent more and more time away from home, from high school through grad school, I went to church less and less frequently. I only went when I came back home. I liked sleeping in on Sundays, waking up to make pancakes and watch sports, like Pops did. I liked not feeling obligated to sit through hours of song and lecture that, as a child, I couldn't possibly be able to understand or relate to, or grab some kind of significant meaning from. It's ironic that an Intro to Biblical Literature class at a catholic university taught me to scrutinize Christianity more carefully. I contemplated questions like, "Wait a minute, you mean religion is a man-made construct meant to keep people in line? There're three creation stories? Which one is true? Is one truer than the others? The *people* in power and the *politics* of the time the books were written influenced religion? What exactly are we supposed to have faith in?"

My skepticism increased. I never stopped believing in God, but I stopped putting my faith in people, and even when they had good intentions, I wondered if they really understood their own beliefs.

The atmosphere of the sermons at my church changed over the years. Church was usually laid back, at best, and typical, protestant boredom at worst. But the sermons began to take on the fervor of a southern revival, complete with whoopin', hollerin', screamin', and faintin'.

'Yes, Lawd. Yes Lawd. Hallelujah. Thank you Jesus, thaaaank you Jesus. Yesss lawd. Jeeeeezus.'

That shit used to scare the hell out of me as a kid. As an adult, I can appreciate the fact that people are just expressing overwhelming feelings of joy. Or whatever. But when I thought I caught a whiff of bullshit, it made me more resentful than I already was. It seemed fake and insincere to me, like some people just wanted everybody to know how down they were with JC, regardless of whether or not they acted like real Christians Monday through Saturday. It got to a point that every time I was about to enter church, my nerves would start rattling.

My skepticism and lack of excitement about being in church prevented me from joining in on the action, often making me look and feel like a stiff. Not that I was ever the only one, but sometimes it seemed like the reverend was talkin' straight to me.

He'd say things like, "Come on y'all, there's nothing wrong with shoutin' fuh Jesus. You can shout when John Starks hits a basket fuh the Knicks. Why cant'cha shout fuh Jesus? If you didn't come here to praise Jesus, then what'cha come here fuh?" It was a question I asked myself every time I walked into that sanctuary.

Moms and I talked about matters of faith on several occasions, often during times when I was still unsure of what the concept of "God" meant to me. Sometimes it left her with the feelin' that she somehow failed in her quest to raise me as God-fearing. I could only assure her that there was nothing wrong with my up bringing and that as an adult, it was my right and responsibility to deal with faith the way I saw fit. She respected this and respected the fact that I had reservations about the direction our church had taken.

The only times I ever went to church as an adult was when Moms asked me to. I went reluctantly, thinking that I'd make the most of it by actually listenin' to the sermons and comparing them to how I saw the picture. All the while, my nerves rattled. I could barely contain my cynicism of organized religion and the inherent exclusiveness of believing that Jesus is the one and only savior of the world, and of the hypocrisy that runs through a so-called Christianity that is similar to that of America's so-called democracy.

On a more personal level, the thought of going to church usually put a damper on my Saturday nights. I couldn't get too drunk or stoned; I might not be able to wake up and ask for forgiveness.

I thought about the situation from all angles. There was the angel on one shoulder, the good son, who felt guilty for not wanting to comply with Moms' occasional request to accompany her to church. She never asked me for anything. All she wanted was for me, by all accounts her only family contact at that time, to join her in what she's built as the foundation of her life, the bedrock that keeps her goin', and to show gratitude for all the things we should've been grateful for, including my education.

But I was goin' through this other shit. The dark angel on the other shoulder was fuckin' with me, makin' me doubt the use of it all; church, school, everything this society is built on. After the reunion, I couldn't find a single thing to have faith in. I wanted to explode on everything.

"Finish school for me."

"Lie if you have to."

"You're twenty-five now. What the hell are you doin'? Are you makin' your own decisions or are you gonna keep doin' what mommy tells you to do? Look where it's gotten you so far. Are you doing things for her or for yourself?"

The devils and angels met on Mother's Day, two weeks after the ABC reunion.

I don't remember not goin' to church with Moms on Mother's Day, unless I was away at school. It was implicit, expected, and understood.

But I woke up that Sunday wonderin' if I was gonna go. I heard her bustling around the apartment as I was half-asleep on the couch. She usually had to be at church about an hour before actual service because of choir rehearsal. She usually drove ahead, and I took the train later. If I left the house by 11 a.m., I could make it just in time for the start of service. But that morning, I was pissy, hung-over, and still embittered about the reunion.

As she headed out the door, her perfume waded through the apartment, a scent I always associated with Sunday morning church. There was no, "See you in a little bit" like there usually was, or any discussion at all, as I pretended to be asleep on the couch in the living room.

That previous week, we hadn't talked about church. She knew I didn't like goin'. I told her that I'd take her out to dinner the following Tuesday since the restaurants would be packed that Sunday. I was satisfied that that would be our little Mother's Day celebration.

At 11 a.m., long after she left the house, I took a few tokes of weed, sat by the window that overlooked the garden behind the apartment building, and anxiously enjoyed the pleasant Sunday morning.

I had come down from being stoned by 2:30 p.m. I sat stolidly in front of the TV, not watching the sports program that was on. I was trying to persuade myself that she knew how I felt about church and that we would be celebrating her day on another day, and that she'd be cheery after a good service. But I knew what I was doing. I had to do it, but it didn't keep me from tremblin' with guilt and sadness.

I noticed our cat run toward the door. She heard Moms' keys jingling down the hallway well before I did. My eyes were glued to the TV as she opened the door. She entered soundlessly, not making eye contact with me.

I said, "Hey," trying to sound normal.

"Hi."

"How was church?"

"Service was fine. Your *card* was beautiful..." Pause.

"What's wrong?"

"Nothing."

"Obviously somethin's wrong..."

No answer. I sat up in front of the TV now, forearms resting on my knees, my shoulders achingly stiff. I don't know how long I sat there like that. It might've been minutes or hours. I was tryin' to figure out a way to get this started, because whether I could control it or not, it was about to come out. Finally, she came directly into the living room to retrieve something. I asked what seemed to be the dumbest question ever.

"Are you mad that I didn't go this morning?"

"I'm not as mad as I am hurt..."

And then it started. She threw up her hands in surrender and cried, trying to shuffle quickly out of the living room. I tried to establish a measure of strength and control over the situation and myself. I commanded her to come into the living room and sit across from me.

And then I started up. She hadn't seen me cry like that since pop's funeral. I don't know what hurt more: the unspoken, unacknowledged troubles on my mind for all those years, the fact that I hurt her, or the fact that I out-cried her. My breakdown came in torrents. The delay switch finally broke, and everything inside came out on her. I was disgusted with myself. I was disgusted with ABC and the idea she planted in my mind that it would all mean something to me some day. The confusion of my experiences and the feeling that I had been lied to blinded me from seeing that benefit. For ten years I got caught up in a river of opportunity, barely having had time to come up for air, not having a true sense of who or where I was. I hadn't developed into the person I wanted to be because I was lured and distracted by the chase for things and the pressure of social acceptance. If only I had listened to myself back in high school, when I knew I didn't want to go to college, maybe I'd have saved myself from the bullshit and found a different, more satisfying path. Instead, I always felt this constant pressure to choose: choose a school, choose a career, choose this, choose that, black or white, upper-class values or "keeping it real" loyalty, not mention a life tied to debt. I had no sense of belonging, to myself, or to anything or anyone. I had been living life with no real feeling, no real passion, no real sense of purpose. I felt shut down and alienated. I was living in constant delay mode. I played that fucking game and it left me empty and reeling, like a wound-up go-bot. I felt alone in my own world, struggling with concepts of who I was and what I was meant to do with my life. I felt like nobody understood that, despite degrees and accolades, I felt shut down and alienated to protect myself from the barrage of ignorance from the two worlds I traversed, black and white, all for pursuits that could never have fulfilled me the way the answer to that question I was lookin' for would. I finally told her that I felt completely fucked up and angry, and that in some way, I blamed her.

I purposely hurt Moms but released ten years worth of housed frustration, the numbness relieved like circulation returning to my limbs in pins and needles.

didn't want her to feel bad, but I wanted her to finally understand where the hell I was coming from. I knew she wasn't to blame for my angst. She had only done what any thoughtful, caring parent would do: push their children to excel, to pursue avenues that they themselves didn't have when they were coming up. She had nothin' but my best interests in mind. What decent parent wouldn't want the best for their kids? How was she supposed to know that I harbored so much resentment and feelings of emptiness despite my academic success? I had buried those thoughts and feelings all those years and a cauldron brewed inside until it finally poured out on her lap.

I don't know how long we bumbled and stumbled through explanations and sobs, but when my whining was over, we agreed that it was good that our Mother's Day episode turned out the way it did. She had no idea I was holding all that in for so long. But my anger was indeed misplaced. My breakdown softened the disillusionment I felt after the reunion. Deep down, I'd rather have had parents who pushed me to excel rather than leave me to the whim of a dirty world. Token program or not, ABC has broadened horizons for over twenty-five years worth of candidates, including myself. At least I had a chance to experience the chase for the "American Dream" from the inside, whether or not I choose to pursue it. At least I have a choice, and given my education and experiences, I still have a chance to take the profitable road down the dark side of company life and the middle-class, bu-jee ass illusion of material success. What the fuck is there for me to whine about?

Maybe I was more angry at the society that created a need for a program like ABC to begin with, a system that breeds ignorance between people who have more in common than not. Maybe I was angry at our assembly-line educational system that encourages us to see ourselves as products in the corporate market more than as human beings in development. Maybe I was just pissed at the world and that I hadn't quite found my place in it.

Out of an act of malicious anger, I was able to understand that I was already everything my folks had hoped for. All they ever asked was that I did my best, nothing more. I wanted to do more, but I no longer confused the terms. I could do whatever I wanted. But when all was said and done, I needed a kind of confirmation from the one person whose efforts steered me in the direction my life took. No matter how grown-up I thought I was, Moms' opinion and understanding mattered to me, perhaps the only opinion that really mattered. Was I weird for not wanting to use my education for a fast, empty corporate track? Was I weird for not wanting to become some bu-jee ass, middle-class carbon copy? Was I weird for being a peppershaker with a pinch of salt, not conforming to these notions we're supposed to keep about what's "black" or "white?" Was my poor, educated black ass a disappointment?

It was clueless, momma's boy nonsense. I hadn't lost anything by traversing the black/white divide through ten years of higher learning. I was relieved to hear her say that I was still the same son she knew before I left the Bronx, and the only thing that changed was my ability to excel, compete, accomplish and survive, no matter what the environment or the circumstances. There was nothing wrong with me for wanting to break out, break free, to live my life on my own terms. It was up to me to take what I had learned and steer the course of my life. If I wanted to go crazy, I could do it. I had to remind myself that I was my own person, my own man, and the fulfillment of what Pops made Moms promise him on his deathbed.

Her encouragement helped me to realize that I had her blessing to be whatever it was I wanted to be, to live whatever I was about with whomever I choose. She helped me liberate myself in a sense I hadn't previously felt. I was free to discover what was truly inside of me, buried under the weight of my own angst, and under our limited social concepts of who we are and how we live.

Our relationship changed dramatically after that day. Our communication became more than just mother/son chit-chat. I officially became a self-sufficient adult with particular ideas and a particular point of view of myself and the world, and it was perfectly okay, perfectly normal. The parent releases the child into the world, her job done. The child releases himself from the parent, free to live his life. That was the day I really grew up, the day I accepted responsibility for my own fate, free from anyone's ideals but my own.

For better or for worse, I was born to Richard and Timmie Wright, was granted a scholarship to a program that gave me a chance to play out these games we play, and was molded into who I am, whatever that may be. It took a little while, but I found that semblance of freedom. I felt giddy, like I was a little kid again, expecting Star Wars toys on Christmas, imagining what the next battle was gonna be.

About a month later, I gave the speech at church, the one where a nod turned into a promise. I don't remember what it was called. Something to do with "Double." It wasn't the rant I thought it would be, but I remember a lot of folks tellin' me afterwards that it was powerful and compelling, and that I had the complete, undivided attention of the congregation. I don't remember much of it myself, besides givin' the whole schpeel about how difficult it was to go away to school, the social situation, yadda yadda yadda.

I know that at the end of the speech, my general message to the kids of the church was that if they weren't livin' the life they wanted to live and pursuing the things that made them happy, then they weren't on the right path, the God-given path, and it wouldn't matter how much education they had. Education is a tool that could be used wisely to pursue the soul's calling, but it could just as easily tool them.

I gave my only copy of the speech to young man on his way to Howard University, knowin' that I didn't have another copy. I didn't need it anymore.

A couple of months after that, a wealthy friend of mine from Georgetown flew me out to Los Angeles. It was the first time I felt anxiety free in a long, long time. He rented a convertible Chevy Malibu for me to kick around town while he was at work.

On a misty, California summer afternoon, I drove up the Pacific Coast Highway, top down, until I came across a weird rock formation above the ocean. I pulled over, parked the car safely, nestled myself into a nook of large rocks, lit a phat joint, threw on my headphones to the sound of Underworld's "Born Slippery," watched sea gulls glide above the waters, felt the cool mist of crashing waves cascade all over my body, and I dreamt up a small list of goals for a short-term future, the first being to get the hell up from under Moms.

If you're reading this now, then I suppose I reached the last goal on that list.

Alan: You Learn

"Initially, I was pretty calm about gettin' laid off [from Leap, his first job out of ad school]. I was somewhat relieved that they let me go at the beginning of the day. Every minute in that place was excruciatingly painful. So I was like, 'Fuck, I can leave? Phew! I can go home. It's a nice day out. Fuck it.'

"Of course, around the second or third day, it sorta set in. People were callin' me and shit. The worst of it all was that all my peers from school knew about it. I didn't give a fuck about Leap people, 'cuz they weren't shit anyway. But all my school buddies found out about it, like, instantly. That bummed me out 'cuz I was the star of my class. I worked very hard to establish that equity. That matters. It may only be an ego thing now, but down the line, three years from now, when people start getting power positions, my rep is very important, know what I mean? Because they're makin' decisions now.

"So, it just pissed me off 'cuz I know there was a lot of envy, as there always is when you're successful. And a lot of people out there LOVED to hear the fact that I got laid off. I was the first to get a job, and I was the star pupil. And the way it works with these ad schools, there's a lot of celebrity status that goes along with it. There're the people that are considered stars. They get all the attention from the teachers, all the opportunities. I got sent to New York to represent the school. Everybody was pissed about that. They'd say things like, 'Why does he get to go? That motherfucka gets everything.'

"So now it's like they're saying, 'Oh, ain't that a trip. He got laid off. Ha! Aw shit!' I knew motherfuckas were happy about that shit.

"But I refused to let anybody see me defeated, you know what I mean? I was very cool about it with everybody I spoke to about it. I wasn't gonna say, 'Leap was full of shit anyway.' I was like, 'Cool. I was the first to get a job, it only seems appropriate that I be the first to lose a job, ya know?' I said all the little platitudes I could think of: 'Well, in advertising, you haven't really made it 'til you've lost at least one job. So I've already got that outta the way,' just to show people I wasn't defeated by this thing, because they're gonna have to go through it, too. At some point, you DO have to go through that shit. Someone's gonna lose an account, and you gotta leave. A lot of things can happen.

"But almost immediately, I noticed that this was a blessing 'cuz I started showing my portfolio around, and people were biting at it. I remembered the same sort of glory I felt when I was coming out of ad school. I have a good portfolio. And you know what? That gets you shit. And I had totally forgotten. All this time I been thinking I'm a hack over at Leap. As much as I don't want to believe that on a rational level, on an emotional level, you begin to internalize that shit when motherfuckas treat you like a child. I was like, 'Fuck these motherfuckas. I SHOULD'VE got out of that motherfucka a long time ago.' It took some type of rude awakening like this to get my ass outta there. And if it took me getting laid off, so be it.

"So I didn't work for two weeks. I sent my portfolio to ten places, four or five in San Francisco, the rest in Chicago. My partner at Leap was also laid off but got *an offer over at Leo Burnett. He needed a partner, so that's how I came in. But even that wasn't cool after a while. Leo Burnett has such a bad reputation amongst creatives. It epitomizes the big agency that doesn't do creative work.*

"When I was interning, I thought Leo Burnett was the place to be. When I left there, my whole reason was to get a portfolio and then go back and work at Leo Burnett. But that's completely changed, to the point where they were recruiting me to come over there, gave me scholarship money, two five-hundred dollar checks when I was in school, all this shit, and I was like, 'I don't wanna have anything to do with y'all.' They sent me to New York twice. There were a lot of perks that I amassed, but I worked for it. I didn't feel guilty, and anybody who does, get your shit together, know what I'm sayin'?

"It felt like some kind of weird consolation prize, goin' back to Leo Burnett. I never wanted to go back. Even though it was temporary, I just kept thinking about what my peers were thinking about me. 'I hear Alan's over at Leo. You believe that shit?' That's like the graveyard. You are selling out if you work at Leo Burnett. Despite whether that's true or not, that IS the perception you get as a creative. Problem is, most people at Leo have been there so long, they're oblivious to the outside world, and it doesn't matter. But if you have a creative instinct, and you're at fucking Leo Burnett? Wow!

"But I was gettin' paid so much money, ya know? While I was there, I impressed people, and people liked us. They kept movin' us to different groups, and people were sweating us. I was like, 'This is cool. I'm havin' more fun and enjoying my work here far more than I did at Leap. This is supposed to be a horrible place to be?'

"A lot of times, I think I got laid off from Leap because I wasn't loud enough. No one noticed me. That's bullshit because I know I proved myself. I know my work was good. But because they don't know good work and talent when they see it, they look at other shit.

"Then I got to hearing about shit goin' down at Leap, about other motherfuckas gettin' laid off, losing accounts, and that gave me satisfaction. They've laid off about ten people since I left. When they get one of the people in charge of accounts, you know some shit's fucked up. I get sort of a perverted satisfaction knowin' about how bad things are over there, but part of me feels bad about it.

"Still, in general, I feel good. I've gained my confidence back. Being at Leap for six months killed my confidence in general. The laying off thing was just icing on the cake. Working for hacks and having hacks judge me; I stopped being a good writer. It was just something I couldn't deal with. It was such a blow to my ego. My partner put it best. It's like dating a fat, ugly girl just to get some sex, pass the time, and then have her dump your ass. Damn, ya know? It's fucked up.

"Ultimately, I feel like I've got what I deserve. I'm a good guy. I never fucked anybody over. I could probably stand to be a little bit mean at times. But bein' a good guy, I would have never even gotten my new job in Minneapolis had I not been a good guy. Talent is just the price of entry.

"They fly you out and have you meet everybody to see what your personality's like. And they do a little background check on you to make sure you ain't got no skeletons, 'cuz, their attitude is, 'we don't want nobody up here who's gonna be an

asshole.' So if I weren't a nice guy, I would've been X'd right out of the runnin.

"I feel fulfilled. I feel like my work got me where I am now, and my personality got me where I am. I finally got a job that I can feel proud of, that I know I'm gonna do good work in, that I know is gonna get me respect. If I work hard, which I already know I'm gonna do, after two or three years, I can do whatever the fuck I want, go to any agency I want, make any kinda money I want. I won't have to worry about it again.

"By the way, I love this song [Alanis Morrisette's "Learn"]. She's talkin' about, 'I recommend walkin' around yo' house, with no clothes on, 'cuz when you do that, YOU LEARN.' You bleed, YOU LEARN. You learn not to do that shit no more. You walk, you learn, so LIVE LIFE. Do some shit, 'cuz you ain't gonna learn shit if you don't do somethin', know what I'm sayin'?"

The Meaning of Adversity

"And the mind that has conceived a plan of living must never lose
sight against the chaos which that pattern was conceived.

Ralph Ellison
Epilogue, *Invisible Man*

Alan and I finished our taped conversations sometime around late February,
early March 1998. Afterward, I began transcribing the tapes to writing, then from
writing to the typed page, when I was lucky enough to have Alan's laptop computer
to work on. It was a tedious process. I hadn't even begun to think about putting
our discussions into a coherent form.

I smoked a lot of pot to get through the boredom of the fist stage of putting
this thing together. One evening, while I was in the midst of a particularly bad
cold, I smoked too much weed, to the point where I was extremely dehydrated. I
had trouble breathing, and my throat closed up on me when I tried to guzzle water.
It was the first time I felt like I had lost control over my body. I was scared, which
made my heart beat faster, which made me feel worse. I ran outside to get a breath
of the cold Chicago winter air. It didn't help. I went back upstairs and calmly
explained my situation to Alan, who had just sat down to dig into a meal he prepared
for himself after a long day at work.

I said, "I don't mean to scare you, man, but I think I need to go to the emergency
room. I can barely breathe." He handled it relatively well. He put his food down,
grabbed his car keys, and we were on our way. The ride over to Cook County
Hospital was an eternity of fear. My breathing became more and more labored,
which made me more and more scared, which made my heart beat faster and faster,
which made me feel worse and worse.

The line at check-in was short, but the emergency room was packed full of
people who looked defeated, mostly black. When I got to the counter, I tried to
emphasize to the lady that I could barely breathe and felt like I was gonna pass out.

"Do you have asthma, or any medical condition that brings this on," she asked.

"Uh, no… But I think I just smoked some bad weed." I don't know why I said
that.

"Is there such a thing as good weed? You need to leave that stuff alone. Fill
out these forms. When you're done, have a seat and wait for your name to be
called," she continued.

Feeling like I just got whacked on the nose like a bad puppy, I filled out the
forms, praying that I wouldn't pass out, and then I fell into a seat. I accepted the
situation. I figured, well, if I do pass out, at least I'm already here. I looked around
the room to see what condition everyone else seemed to be in. Nothing major. No
blood streaming from anyone's face, no broken bones, or wails of pain. There was
no hurry. I sank, realizing why everyone looked so defeated.

My breathing was fucked up, but I still felt the pleasure of bein' stoned. My
senses were sensitive to everything around me. I let my thoughts go from my heart

and lungs to the scene around me, turning it into a surreal, bad sitcom. Then I started beating myself up for once again not sticking with my resolve to quit smoking pot. It didn't make me work better or faster, and this time, it helped to land me in a crowded emergency room. I thought that maybe that was someone or something's way of reminding me about my resolve to quit. I told Alan that this time was definitely it for me, the same way a drunk promises not to drink again while his face is hovering over a toilet bowl after a night of mixing drinks. He'd heard it from me before.

A song was playing on a television show on the monitors around the room. It struck me pleasantly, probably in a way that it wouldn't if I wasn't stoned. I asked Alan if he knew what song it was. He started laughing.

"'Addicted,' by a group called K's Choice," he said and laughed. I giggled to tears. It was better than fiction.

I noticed a vagrant lookin' man meandering around the waiting room. He looked like an older, scruffy-bearded, hobo version of Prince. He wore a tattered, Dr. Seuss-type winter hat, and big, block sunglasses, the kind old people wear. He'd sit down next to someone and start a conversation, only for him or her to shortly get up and walk away. I knew I was next.

He sat down on my left, while Alan was on my right, barely containing his laughter. The guy opened up a newspaper and began glazing over the pages like the cliché old, suburban white guy at the breakfast table, humming to himself. After a few minutes, he said something to me. I wasn't paying attention. The whole situation was just too surreal for me to take seriously. I was high, I thought I was gonna pass out, I had no medical insurance, and this old Prince-lookin' motherfucker was talkin' to me. I started to giggle even more, and I closed my mouth inward to keep from bursting. I felt the eyes of the entire waiting room on me. The man wouldn't stop talking. The more I tried to contain my giggle, the more I smirked, and the more confident he became. His tone was flirty in a non-sexual way. I felt my left shoulder creeping away from his persistence, like a junior high school girl on a first date. Eventually, I caved in. I didn't have the will to shoo him away.

He went from flirty to serious in a nano-second. With his beard hangin' just above my shoulder, he asked me, in a deep voice, "Do you know the meaning of adversity?"

I turned to look at him briefly, my giggle spell abruptly broken. He lowered his head so that he could see me with un-shaded eyes. They seemed to sparkle and whirl. They were strange, but then again, I was stoned. I quickly looked away and feigned a faint smile. I knew everyone was lookin' at me, and I just wanted to get him away.

I said, "I'm sure I don't." My tone indicated that I had had enough of him. He went back to his newspaper. After a few minutes, he got up and sat down next to a little Hispanic girl, cooing and flirting with her.

I don't know how long Alan and I sat there, but the waiting room didn't seem to get any emptier. We spent most of the time shakin' our heads and quietly laughing, mostly at me, for landing us in that weird situation. Before long, my breathing returned to normal, and I felt better. I didn't bother waiting around for my name to be called.

"Fuck it," I said. "Let's get outta here."

I still smoke pot, but the experience left me with a lingering notion that a new phase of my life was beginning, and that it wouldn't be easy. My encounter with the vagrant-Prince man seemed too strange to be mere coincidence. I felt like I was getting a clue from a divine messenger. I knew what adversity meant in the general sense: having to overcome something. I was too embarrassed by the scene to give his question serious thought at the time he asked. Later on, however, whether the whole thing was coincidence or not, the message became clear.

I looked up Webster's definition of adversity: "A state of affliction or hardship: Misfortune."

It took about three years for this book to go from concept to a first publishing, so that was the beginning of my understanding of adversity. While I was writing this book, I worked a job that I absolutely hated in the mailroom of a prestigious advertising company. I used the excuse that I didn't really want a job that required a lot of investment on my part because I was so busy trying to put this together. But I still felt a sense of degradation, having to answer to an uneducated, "white trash" overseer and some pompous executives while pushing a mail cart, struggling to make ends meet with pithy paychecks, and feeling the cold bite of the starving-artist lifestyle. I personally came to know everything Alan and I had talked about: the dynamics of race and class in corporate America, the assumptions many people made about those of us who worked in the mailroom (mostly black and from the South Side), and the emptiness of 9 to 5 living.

Eventually, a woman by the name of Jane Cole snatched me out of the abyss of the mailroom, promoting me into a department that put me a step closer to the possibility of a career in advertising. And it wasn't a charity thing, either. She recognized something different in me than the others in the mailroom, the intangible social currency that ABC gave people like me, the quality that opens the doors for those of us educated in white academia. But after a year, I still couldn't shake the urge not to succumb to a job that was…just a job, something less than what I sincerely cared about. I didn't give a fuck about making commercials for McDonalds or that swill known as Budweiser. I didn't want a career in advertising. My book was finished, my friends were slowly trickling out of Chicago, and I had nothing or no one keeping me there.

Then 9/11 happened. As trite as this may sound, I took away from that world-shattering event a profound sense of urgency for finding the things that were important to me in life. That included being closer to the people I loved back East. So, again, with no real plan in mind, I quit a cushy but mind-numbing job and moved to Connecticut, for as much as I love my peeps in New York, there was still something about New York City living that didn't beckon me home. New York will always be special to me, but once you break out outta there, there's no going back.

Still not quite knowing what I wanted to do with my life, I spent a year waiting tables at a seafood restaurant, the most un-enjoyable job I've ever had. It's amazing how far we can stretch our tolerance for things we thought we'd never do. I was one of those people who said, "I could never wait tables." I was pretty miserable during that stretch, but eventually I found my way into a newspaper as a circulation assistant. Within three months I was hired to write for a weekly. Within a year and a half, I became an editor. And I teach part-time at a community college in Waterbury, finally giving in to that old notion, and I can't say that I don't enjoy it.

Besides wrapping up the tail end of this story, just in case you were wondering what became of me, I say all of this to note that I have indeed become very intimate with the meaning of adversity; there have been many ups and downs during this time, mostly downs. I no longer doubt that the old man in that emergency room in Chicago was an emissary, whether he knew it or not, from that higher power we refer to as God. I started on a new path as a seeker, and the life of a seeker ain't easy. We idealize. We don't settle for less than what we consider divine. We don't accept the programmed reality of the matrix. We don't accept that anything's impossible. We are the dreamers that dare to dream. But there are no guarantees, which make disappointment that much bitter, inducing doubt, challenging our faith that we will one day find that thing we're looking for. To look for answers is to live with adversity. But there's a genuine passion for living life the way you want to live it that comes from searching, even if you haven't quite reached that goal yet. It intensifies all other feelings, giving a sense that you're really living life beyond the drudgery of conforming to something that you ain't feelin'.

I started this new journey with the intention of looking for something: call it happiness, self-awareness, security, ambition, the ideal lifestyle; call it what you will. The question mark that built itself inside my head started to fade, but it's still there, in a different way. I don't have the same urgency I had when I started this book to find the words to formulate that question. I hope this isn't too disappointing, but the fact is, I still don't know what the hell I was lookin' for, what I am looking for.

The elusive question was the real affliction, but I found out that the search for that question only created more, and they don't stop. If they did, then perhaps I'd have put the ultimate question on the table. Perhaps I'd have found the ultimate answer. Perhaps it would've been the ultimate disappointment, then what? I've settled into the permanence of the search for that thing I'm lookin' for, born from a perpetual question mark in the brain. The search is ongoing, the questions unending. The trip is permanent.

Breaking out is the first step, breaking free from the limitations we impose on ourselves based on our experiences, limitations encouraged by an environment that just wants us to play along and don't ask questions. Just asking the questions is monumental. If we did that of ourselves, perhaps we could start asking questions of those forces that steer the course of our society, the forces that have most of us living check to check without guaranteed health insurance, accepting a standard of living that pales in comparison to that of other developed nations, frustrated by the politics of lesser evils, waging campaigns for questionable pursuits that devastate the lives of thousands.

But it's scary to hold that mirror up, to examine what we're really made of, the things that brought us to where we are as individuals and as a society. It can be depressing to dig up those demons and keep them at bay once they're acknowledged. And once those questions arise, once we swallow the red pill [like Neo in The Matrix], there's no turning back. We begin to chart our own course, having no idea where it's going to take us.

Instead, many of us succumb to that fear of the unknown and settle into the life that we've taken for granted. We stay in our pods, accepting that things are the way they are, and that there's nothing we can do to change them. We grab at fleeting pleasures that mimic happiness, believing that we can't dare to imagine a better way of living, a better way of governance, a better way of understanding and accepting each other, a better way of resolving conflict, something more than what's been drilled into us since the day we were born. We're not encouraged to search. We're encouraged to obey. And so things don't change.

I know fully well that it seems pointless to raise these points without offering solutions. Most of us are too busy strivin' to survive and don't have the luxury of dreaming up a better concept of life. But it can't hurt to ask questions, to search within our own heads for something more than survival.

It was the search that propelled me forward all along. It doesn't matter if empty chases, unrealistic ideals, my limitations, or the limitations of others stunted my sight. The better I know myself, the easier my search becomes. Maybe if we all got to know ourselves a little better, we can extend that into our world, daring to come up with something better than what we have. I accept that some questions may never be answered, but the questions are the path. The journey along that path becomes invigorating, injecting feeling and faith into life that there's nowhere to go but forward. We are as we are, whatever that may be, whatever happened to make us this way, whatever we may be doing, whatever we're searching for. To search is to live. It's the only way to live. It's the only way to become. It's the only way to overcome adversity.

Note:
    Alan now lives in Amsterdam, a confirmed pot-head, working at a small advertising firm.

About the Author

Lerron Richard Wright was born in New York City and raised in the Bronx. In 1993, he received his bachelor's degree in English from Georgetown University in Washington, D.C. Three years later, he earned a master's degree in Educational Media from Fairfield University in Connecticut.

Still undecided about a career, Wright moved to Chicago, where he lived for four years. There, he worked on his first novel *Breakout: A Search for Being* while pushing a mail cart for a prestigious advertising company. When his novel was completed, Wright moved back east to Connecticut, not content to stay in any one place for too long. He now lives in Branford and works as an editor for the *Milford Weekly*, while also teaching part-time at Naugatuck Valley Community College in Waterbury.

Also available Summer/Fall 2004 from Fine Tooth Press:

Fiction

Pressure Points by Craig Wolf
Hardboiled Egg by Oscar De Los Santos
The Massabesic Murders by Gypsey Teague
To Beat a Dead Horse by Bill Campbell
White River by Will Bless

Non-Fiction

Spirits of Texas and New England by Oscar De Los Santos

Poetry

Composite Sketches by Lou Orfanella
Balloons Over Stockholm by James R. Scrimgeour

In the Works:

Trickster Tales by JP Briggs
A Poet's Guide to Divorce by David Breedan
Reel Rebels edited by Oscar De Los Santos
Street Angel by Martha Marinara
The New Goddess: Transgendered Women in the Twenty-First Century edited by Gypsey Teague

For more information about these and other titles, as well as author bios and interviews and more, visit us on the web at:

http://www.finetoothpress.com

Printed in the United Kingdom by
Lightning Source UK Ltd., Milton Keynes
138210UK00002B/183/A